Recipes

AND

Messipes

EDITED BY BEN NEWTON

ISBN No: **978-1-0880-0875-1**
Library of Congress Control Number: **2021924437**

Publisher:
Ben Newton
5408 Avenida Cuesta NE
Albuquerque, New Mexico, 87111
sites.google.com/view/RecipesAndMessipes

Book design by Ben Newton.
Printed by IngramSpark.

To my family.
May you always enjoy the great food,
and the messes.

Thank you to all those contributing recipes from the
Newton, Robinson, Poulsen, Schultz, Trent, Burge,
Frank, Jacobs, Emerson, and Koeven Families.
A special thanks, as well, to Amy Koeven for writing
the preface, and helping give the book a theme.
Most importantly, thank you to my wife Erin Newton
for her patience, love, and assistance with this project.

Contents

Preface

WE'VE ALL SEEN recipe books before. We know what a recipe is. Instructions, measurements, careful sequential orderings of tasks, adjustments and substitutions... all are evidence of careful testing and many rounds of trial and error. We benefit from the wisdom yielded from such efforts, and move on with our lives, perfect pancakes in hand. We rarely see the disasters that came before. This recipe book, written by a crowd of people, is different. Through the stories attached to many of the recipes, we get to see behind the curtain. We get to see not just the recipe, but the messipe, the mess that (eventually) gave us the recipe.

The origin of the messipe begins with a picture of a chocolate cake. I was six years old, looking through my mother's Lion House Cookbook. There was this double layer chocolate cake that I thought was beautiful. (Clean lines... delightful!) Mom noticed me with this cake picture, and I told her how badly I wanted to make something like that. She decided we could do that, just the two of us. We made a plan, bought chocolate together, and everything. I remember her teaching me how to make the frosting and letting me lick the beaters of the mixer. I was so proud when we served that cake.

That was the first time I knew that baking is in my soul. What I lack in skill, I make up for in enthusiasm. When I get an idea, it sticks until I've baked it. Results are... mixed. There was that Amish bread when I was 13; Dad told me it would get me a husband. Fast forward a few years, and I was living with Ben and Erin in North Carolina. Erin and I were each baking a cookie recipe while Ben worked (and chimed in with fraction help as needed). My cookies turned out half burned and half raw, but I've never laughed so hard. By the end of the night, we had coined the term "messipe."

Various messipes have followed. There was the checkerboard cake that ended up in crumbs, and me crying on the kitchen floor. There was the smores cake that did not toast as planned. That time the cake ended up on the floor rather than me. There was the time Matthew asked for a "chocolate fire cake" and I learned how not to temper chocolate, but it sure looked like chocolate fire when I was done. When Wilder and I got married, we started trying to replicate things from the Great British Baking Show.

Florentines ended up delicious, and laminated dough, three times in a row, was mostly a waste of several pounds of butter, but I loved every minute of it.

I've learned something from all the failures that end with me or cake or chocolate all over the floor. A recipe that turns out well is enjoyable in the moment, but a messipe, well, that's a story that will live forever. Either way, you get something good. This thought is such a comfort to me while I am stuck in the kitchen. If I'm stressed now, it usually means a good story later. If it turns out well, then... yum. As long as you get one of those options, you're good. Eventually, messipes turn into recipes that work every time (which was a comforting thought when I accidentally made grapefruit butter in the pursuit of macarons).

I am thrilled to read and use this recipe book, because it magically combines messipes, recipes, and masterpieces of family lore. Good recipes mixed with memories and stories! I can't wait to try making Jen's Amazing Potato Rolls, that concentrate generations of wisdom into a single recipe. Sandy's sunshine carrots remind me of Ben and Erin getting married, shelling peas with the Newtons, Stacy giving me all of her attention while we talked about that carrot recipe, which felt big when I was eleven. Amy's Cajun Chicken Pasta recipe reminds me of cooking with her just after Karen was born, and I spent my days snuggling a perfect tiny baby. Libby's section reminds me that she used to wake me up in the morning by putting tiny chocolate chip cookies in my mouth. Bama's Ham Stuffed Potatoes remind me of how relieved and grateful I was when Sandy and Dave came to Erin and Ben's house and fed everyone after Mardee was born. Aunt Becky's contributions from Aunts and Grandmothers along with her own remind me that food is a way that families connect and show love even across generations.

Over time, these messipies improved with the wisdom and experience of generations into the recipes we have in this book. Here we get the benefit of everyone's work, everyone's messes, and everyone's love, bringing us all together. May this book continue bringing us together, to the kitchen.

You know what they say- Women belong in the kitchen. Men belong in the kitchen. Everyone belongs in the kitchen. It's where the food is.

Amy Koeven

Appetizers and Snacks

APPETIZER: /ˈapəˌtīzər/ **n.** The thing that's not too big and not too small. Just right to eat before a meal. Appetizers are great because imagine its right before dinner and you want something to eat right then, but you don't want to overeat before your meal. Then you see the appetizers, the thing that fits your desire. Problem solved!

Quinton Schultz - age 13

SNACKS: Imagine you are watching the super bowl. You may find on the table, the most humble and amazing food ever... SNACKS! Snacks are a type of food that keep you active and not hungry. However, if you eat too much they will spoil your appetite for your next meal. Snacks consist of chips, licorice, nachos, popcorn or little amounts of food, to name a few. Snacks are, sadly, supposed to be eaten in between a meal (like I said) to keep you active. Personally, my favorite snacks are kiwis, pomegranates and watermelon. Snacks are the best part of the day!

Maya Schultz - age 11

Cucumber Boats
makes 2 servings

1 cucumber, peeled
1 cup cottage cheese
Salt and black pepper, to taste

1. Peel cucumber, if desired, slice it in half and scoop out the seeds. Fill each half with about half a cup of low-fat cottage cheese. Top with salt and pepper, to taste.

Recipe courtesy of Libby Newton – from Six Sisters' Stuff

Chicken Pinwheeles
makes 4 servings

4 tortillas
4 spreadable cheese wedges (such as laughing cow cheese)
1 pound deli-sliced chicken breast
4 leaves lettuce
1 cucumber, sliced thin lengthwise

1 tomato, sliced

1. Spread a wedge of spreadable cheese on each tortilla. On each tortilla layer sliced chicken breast, lettuce, cucumber slices, and tomatoes.

2. Roll up each tortilla, and cut into 1 inch slices.

Recipe courtesy of Libby Newton – adapted from Six Sisters' Stuff

Ham (or Turkey) & Swiss Sliders

12 Hawaiian sweet rolls
6 to 9 slices of deli ham or turkey
6 slices of Swiss cheese
¼ cup (½ stick) butter
1 teaspoon mustard (any flavor)
1 teaspoon Worcestershire sauce
1 tablespoon poppy seeds

1. Preheat oven to 350 ° F.
2. DO NOT separate roll, slice all 12 rolls in half at the same time.
3. Cut deli meat and cheese into 1/4ths.
4. On bottom half of rolls, layer 2 to 3 pieces of deli meat onto each roll section.
5. Add 2 pieces of cheese to each roll section.
6. Place top half of rolls back on top.
7. Melt butter, then mix mustard, Worcestershire sauce, and poppy seeds into melted butter.
8. Spread mixture heavily on top and sides of rolls.
9. Place rolls in a greased 9x13 dish.
10. Bake in preheated oven for 10 to 13 minutes or until hot and cheese is melted.
11. Remove from oven and cut into 12 individual sliders.

Recipe courtesy of Jo Jacobs

Food for Thought

Lazy way; Don't cut your deli meat and cheese into 1/4ths and just layer an approximate equivalent amount of meat and cheese on the rolls. Pro - its faster, Con - sliders may not have even amounts, but will still be delicious either way!

Chefnotes

🎩 Great for parties and get-togethers. We also like to make and leave them in the fridge uncooked. We will slice off a few at a time and cook for easy lunchtimes or snacks.
Can be stored in fridge for up to 3 days (but ours usually never last that long).

Slow Cooker Chilli Cheese Dip

makes 8 to 10 servings   prep time: 4 hours   cook time: 3 to 4 hours

1 (15-ounce) can of chili

1 cup salsa

1 (8-ounce) package of cream cheese, room temperature

1 cup shredded cheddar cheese, plus more for garnishing

1 clove of garlic

1 onion, diced

Green onions for garnishing (optional)

1. Spray the ceramic insert of a 3 to 4 quart slow cooker with no-stick cooking spray.

2. Place all ingredients except additional cheese and green onions in slow cooker and mix well. Cook on low 3 to 4 hours or until completely heated through, stirring twice during cooking time.

3. Stir well before serving and top with additional shredded cheese and chopped green onions, if desired.

4. Serve with chips or your favorite crackers or vegetables.

Recipe courtesy of Libby Newton – from Six Sisters' Stuff

CHAPTER 1. APPETIZERS AND SNACKS

Hot Spinach and Artichoke Dip

makes 16 Servings   prep time: 10 minutes

We take this to the Anthony's parents house for Christmas every year. Usually we buy crostini from Harmon's to dip in it. One year I decided to be ambitious and buy a baguette and make my own crostini. Don't do it! It isn't worth it! Cutting it all up, brushing olive oil on one side, broiling it, turning ALL of them over and doing it again. It took forever and wasn't as good as the store-bought crostini.

1 cup thawed, chopped frozen spinach
1½ cups canned chopped artichoke hearts
6 ounces cream cheese
¼ cup sour cream
¼ cup mayonnaise
⅓ cup grated Parmesan
½ teaspoon red pepper flakes

¼ teaspoon salt
¼ teaspoon garlic powder

1. Boil spinach and artichokes in 1 cup of water until tender, then drain. Discard liquid.
2. Heat cream cheese in microwave for 1 minute or until hot and soft.
3. Stir in the remaining ingredients and serve hot.

Recipe courtesy of Rose Frank – adapted from Alton Brown

Chefnotes

We always use our small slow cooker to serve it warm.

Apple Butter

3 quarts (12 cups) cooked apples
½ cup water
¾ cup vinegar
1 tablespoon vanilla extract
1 tablespoon cinnamon
1 teaspoon cloves
6 cups white sugar

Juice of one lemon
1 tablespoon nutmeg
1 tablespoon allspice

1. Peel and core apples, and place in a large pot.
2. Add 1/2 cup water and cook until soft.
3. Add remaining ingredients and cook for 20 minutes.

Recipe courtesy of Rebekah Emerson

Avocado Salsa

1 (29-ounce) can diced tomatoes with garlic and onion
2 fresh tomatoes, diced
1 (11-ounce) can white shoepeg corn, drained
1 (6-ounce) can black olives, chopped
1 bunch green onions, thinly sliced
2 avocados, diced
½ cup Italian dressing
Juice of 1 lime
¼ to ½ cup cilantro, chopped
Salt and pepper, to taste

1. In a large bowl combine all ingredients.
2. Chill overnight and serve with tortilla chips.

Recipe courtesy of Sherry Poulsen

Chefnotes

☞ We use the Del Monte brand of diced tomatoes with garlic and onion, and the Green Giant brand of shoepeg corn.

Anthony's Habanero Mango Salsa
makes about ½ a blender full

*A*nthony joined a salsa subreddit because if he wants to do something, there is a reddit for that. After trying several things out and getting lots of tips about roasting, he made this recipe up and it is so good!

Olive oil, for roasting

1 jalapeño

3 Roma tomatoes

1 onion

1 red bell pepper

1 mango

1 habanero

4 cloves of garlic, not peeled

½ bunch of cilantro

½ lime

Salt and pepper, to taste

1. Prepare a baking pan by lightly spraying olive oil on the surface.

2. Cut the jalapeño, tomatoes, and onion in half. Cut the bell pepper and mango in chunks. Place the jalapeños, tomatoes, onions, bell peppers, mangos, whole habanero (without the stem), and cloves of garlic on the baking pan. The bell peppers and the habanero should be placed on the outside edges as they will char first.

3. Spray ingredients lightly with olive oil.

4. Broil on high until charred to your liking.

5. Remove the garlic and take the skin off with a fork.

6. Blend in blender until very smooth, adding cilantro, juice from 1/2 a lime, and salt and pepper to taste.

7. Refrigerate after and serve when cold.

Recipe courtesy of Anthony Frank

Chefnotes

☞ Make sure you have plenty of chips in the house. Also, don't be afraid to get a good char.

Peanut Butter Energy Bites

2 cups old fashioned oats

1 cup peanut butter

⅔ cup raw, unsalted pumpkin or sunflower seeds

⅔ cup toasted coconut flakes

3 tablespoons mini chocolate chips

⅔ cup honey

2 teaspoons vanilla extract

½ teaspoon sea salt

1. Combine all ingredients and mix well.

2. Roll into one inch balls and store in the fridge or freezer (we prefer the freezer).

Recipe courtesy of Jen Burge

Chapter 2

Breakfast and Brunch

THEY SAY IT'S THE MOST important meal of the day! Is that so? Well then we better do it right!

I'm sure there are a dozen great recipes here, but there is, by and far, one great breakfast meal that tops the list. What's that you say? Well just sit back, nice and easy, and I'll tell you.

Of course all of us have experienced the mad morning rush, with no time to eat. Grab a granola bar or a yogurt or that stale donut you left sitting on the counter three days ago thinking someone will surely eat this. Then running out the door leaving a trail of crumbs or worse! No! Stop! Get up 10 minutes early and sit down to...... drum roll please...... a simply grand, satisfying, stick to your ribs, bowl of......

mush.

Mush? Mush......?

Yes mush. It's calming, soothing, and peaceful. It does not snap, crackle, or pop! It just lies there begging to be eaten and fortifying that hollow in the belly with a warm "Thank you, for making me so happy as I slide down your esophagus and swirl lovingly around your stomach."

No heartburn. No indigestion. Just peace.

Okay? Okay. Breakfast? Yes! Now get to work!!!!

Dave Newton

Deluxe Oatmeal
makes 4 servings

Several years ago a major fast-food chain started started serving oatmeal ... and it was actually quite good, because it was served with dried fruit, nuts, and apples. I decided we could make deluxe oatmeal at home. Rather than cooking the oatmeal in water, I use milk, which results in a yummy, creamy oatmeal.

2 cups quick oats
3½ cups milk
¼ teaspoon salt
<u>Suggested Toppings:</u>
Chopped pecans or other nuts
Cinnamon
Syrup
Brown sugar
Apples, chopped
Berries
Bananas
Dried cranberries

Raisins or other dried fruit

1. Measure the quick oats into a small bowl so it is ready to quickly dump into the milk.
2. Pour the milk into a 4-quart pan (any smaller and the milk will boil over). Mix in the salt, and heat until the milk starts boiling.
3. Immediately add the oats and stir constantly with a wire whisk until you no longer see a top layer of milk, and the oatmeal and milk are fully combined.
4. Pour into serving bowls immediately, scraping out the pan to avoid the oatmeal drying on.
5. Serve warm with any combination of the toppings listed above.

Recipe courtesy of Ben Newton

Marvelous Mush

I have a great family and some really super, fabulous cousins. One of those cousins is Liz Robinson Rich. She has always been patient with me, especially when I was a younger and sometimes awkward tagalong. She has always been gracious and free with her wisdom and advice. I appreciate her.

Well, when she married and became a Rich, her new family hosted a great wedding breakfast. As I understand, it was a continuation of a family tradition. The grandkids in the family would come together on Saturdays and their grandparents would make them a breakfast of waffles, fried spam and (you guessed it) Marvelous Mush! I enjoyed their wedding celebration so much and have held onto this recipe ever since.

Our family has a tradition of having a waffle breakfasts every 6 month on general conference morning. I have incorporated Marvelous Mush into our tradition. Thank you Liz and Burk Rich!

7 cups of boiling water

1¾ cups cornmeal

1½ cups white sugar

4 large eggs

1 cup water

1. In a large pot, bring water to a boil.
2. Meanwhile, in a bowl mix together cornmeal, sugar, water and eggs.
3. Slowly add some of the boiling water to the cornmeal mixture, about 1/3 cup at a time, while stirring.
4. When it is warmed sufficiently, add the mix to the boiling water while whisking. Keep mixing while you bring it back up to a boil.
5. When it is thick and bubbling, take it off the heat and serve.

Recipe courtesy of Erin Newton – from the Rich family

Food for Thought

As I recall, the Rich family serves the marvelous mush with condensed milk. To me it is like eating warm, sweet, sunshine!

Butterscotch Oatmeal

*E*rin can tell you about how I wanted to like yogurt. I also always wanted to like oatmeal. Convenient and healthy, right? It seemed the texture of oatmeal wouldn't allow such a thing, until I found this recipe. The secret is that you use egg. I almost had Aunt Debbie convinced, but egg doesn't get along with her. We like to put diced apple or banana in it.

1 large egg, beaten

1 ¾ cups milk

½ cup packed brown sugar

1 cup rolled oats

2 tablespoons butter

1. In a saucepan over medium heat, whisk together the egg, milk and brown sugar.

2. Mix in the oats.

3. When the oatmeal begins to boil, cook and stir until thick.

4. Remove from the heat, and stir in butter until melted. Serve immediately.

Recipe courtesy of Amy Trent – from www.allrecipes.com/recipe/83853

Baked Oatmeal

When Amelia lived with us she would sometime make baked oatmeal. This is a different recipe than what she made, and likely not as good, but my kids really like it.

3 cups rolled oats
1 cup brown sugar
2 teaspoons ground cinnamon
2 teaspoons baking powder
1 teaspoon salt
1 cup milk
2 large eggs
½ cup melted butter
2 teaspoons vanilla extract

¾ cup dried cranberries, raisins, or frozen berries

1. Preheat oven to 350° F.
2. In a large bowl, mix together oats, brown sugar, cinnamon, baking powder, and salt. Stir in milk, eggs, melted butter, and vanilla extract. Stir in dried fruit or berries. Spread into a greased 9x13 inch baking dish.
3. Bake in preheated oven for 40 minutes.

Recipe courtesy of Ben Newton – from www.allrecipes.com/recipe/51013

Food for Thought

May want to reduce the sugar if want it to be at all healthy.

To-Go Baked Oatmeal

2 large eggs

¼ cup canola oil

1 cup packed brown sugar

½ cup applesauce

1½ cups milk

2 teaspoons vanilla extract

½ teaspoon salt

1 tablespoon ground cinnamon

3 cups old fashioned rolled oats

2 teaspoons baking powder

Your favorite toppings (fruit, nuts, chocolate chips, etc.), optional

1. Preheat the oven to 350° F.

2. Line a muffin tin with paper or paper/foil muffin liners.

3. In a large bowl, whisk the eggs, oil, and brown sugar until sugar is dissolved.

4. Add the applesauce, milk, vanilla, salt, and cinnamon. Whisk until well combined.

5. Stir in the oats and baking powder.

6. Fill each muffin cup with ¼ cup of the oat mixture.

7. If desired, add your favorite toppings. Push the toppings down into the oat mixture with a spoon.

8. Bake for 30 minutes.

9. Let cool for 5 minutes before eating. Store in an airtight container or freeze in a zip top storage bag.

Recipe courtesy of Sandy Newton – adapted from https://www.shamrockfarms.net/recipe/to-go-baked-oatmeal/

Food for Thought

Don't skip the muffin liners for this recipe.

Honey Granola

*D*uring the pandemic I started making recipes that could be made with only ingredients that were fairly easy to store and keep on hand. Besides the oil or butter, and optional nuts and raisins, this granola can be made from ingredients that can be stored for years and years.

4 cups old fashioned rolled oats

1 cup dried cranberries or raisins, optional

2 cups chopped nuts

½ cup coconut oil or butter

¾ cup honey

2 teaspoons cinnamon

½ teaspoon salt

1 teaspoon vanilla extract

1. Preheat oven to 350° F.
2. Mix together the oats, cranberries or raisins and nuts and set aside. In a small pot on medium high heat combine coconut oil, honey, cinnamon, salt, and vanilla. Bring to a boil then reduce heat and boil for 1 minute.
3. Pour the liquid mixture over the oat mixture and stir till combined well.
4. Spread evenly onto a cookie sheet and bake in preheated oven for 20 minutes or until lightly browned, stirring about every 5 minutes.
5. Remove from oven and immediately scrape from pan onto a clean surface.
6. Let the granola cool, then crumble it up and store in an airtight container at room temperature.

Recipe courtesy of Ben Newton – adapted from foodstoragemadeeasy.net

Bama's Best Breakfast Bake

1 can refrigerated crescent rolls

1 (8 to 12-ounce) package sausage

10 to 12 large eggs

1 cup grated cheese

1. Preheat oven to 350° F.
2. Put roll dough in the bottom of a greased 9x13 baking dish.
3. Layer the cooked sausage on top of the dough.
4. Whip up eggs and pour over sausage
5. Then, sprinkle cheese on top.
6. Bake for 30 minutes.

Recipe courtesy of Sandy Newton

Bama's Best Breakfast Bake Bettered by Ben

makes 10 giant pieces

This breakfast recipe has become a staple in our house. My mom introduced us to the recipe, but I think I've perfected it. We made this a lot when Erin had gestational diabetes, because it is fairly low-carb, yet filling. When made right, the crescent rolls magically float up forming a yummy middle layer surrounded by sausage embedded eggs, topped with crisp cheese.

10 sausage links

10 large eggs

1 (8-ounce) can refrigerated crescent rolls

1 cup cheddar jack cheese, grated

1. Preheat oven to 350°F.
2. Arrange frozen sausage links on a plate so they aren't touching. Microwave on high for 1 1/2 to 2 minutes until heated through.
3. Meanwhile, crack the eggs into a large bowl and beat with a wire whisk.
4. Spray the bottom and sides of a 9x13 inch glass baking dish with no-stick spray.
5. Open the can of rolls; unroll each half and spread on the bottom of the baking dish. Don't press down, just lightly set on the bottom of the pan.
6. Cut each sausage link into 6 or 7 pieces and spread on top of the layer of roll dough. Be sure to spread the sausage pieces out evenly.
7. Pour the beaten eggs over the sausage, and then sprinkle with cheese until you can only barely see the sausage, being sure to get the cheese all the way to the sides of the pan.
8. Bake in preheated oven for 30 minutes or until cheese is nicely browned.

Recipe courtesy of Ben Newton

Food for Thought

I highly recommend using original or Vermont maple flavored Banquet Brown 'N Serve Sausage Links. 10 links and 10 eggs seems to be the perfect egg to sausage ratio (not quite as scientific as the onion ratio though. See vegetables chapter.).

When cut into 10 equal pieces, each contains 10 grams of carbohydrates.

Sausage Gravy and Biscuits

*A*ll of my boys love this dish! I always have to double the recipe because they eat it up so quickly. We often eat this for dinner instead of breakfast and I often increase the amounts of spices it calls for.

8 flakey buttermilk biscuits

1 pound sage-flavored pork sausage

2 tablespoons + 1 teaspoon all-purpose flour

2½ cups half and half

1 tablespoon butter

⅛ teaspoon dried thyme

⅛ teaspoon dried crushed rosemary

⅛ teaspoon crushed red pepper flakes

Freshly ground black pepper, to taste

1. Brown sausage in a large saucepan. Use a paper towel to blot out most of the grease from the pan.

2. Add flour, butter, and half and half. Cook on medium-low, stirring often, for several minutes until thickened.

3. Add thyme, rosemary, red pepper flakes and black pepper.

4. Serve over warm biscuits.

Recipe courtesy of Jen Burge

Bacon Egg Muffin Cups

makes 12 egg muffins   prep time: 10 minutes   cook time: 30 minutes

12 slices of bacon

6 slices of wheat bread

12 large eggs

Salt and black pepper, to taste

½ cup cheddar cheese, shredded

¼ cup green onions, sliced

1. Preheat oven to 375 ° F. Spray a muffin tin with nonstick cooking spray.

2. Place a piece of bacon around the inside edge of each muffin cup.

3. Using a small circle cookie cookie cutter cut 12 circles of bread and place one Circle in the bottom of each muffin cup.

4. Crack an egg and empty into a muffin cup on top of the bread. Repeat for all muffin cups.

5. Season with salt and pepper and add a Sprinkle of cheddar cheese. Garnish with sliced green onion.

6. Bake 30 minutes or until egg is set in the middle.

Recipe courtesy of Libby Newton – adapted from Six Sisters' Stuff

Creamed Egg on Toast

makes serves 8 to 12

This recipe became a favorite at our home and we had it at least twice a year on Christmas morning and Easter. When our kids got married and weren't with us on Christmas morning I thought we were through with that tradition, but they wanted to have it for dinner on Christmas when we would meet. So the tradition lives on. I got the recipe from the Better Homes and Garden Cookbook and in the book it has the title of Goldenrod Eggs.

12 Hard-cooked eggs
8 Tablespoons of butter or margarine
½ to ¾ cup all-purpose flour
¾ teaspoon salt
2½ to 3 cups milk
1 cup crumbled bacon (optional)
8 to 12 slices hot buttered toast.

1. Melt butter in saucepan over low heat. Blend in flour, salt and dash of pepper. Add milk and whisk till mixture thickens and bubbles. Peel the eggs and reserve the yokes. Chop up the whites and add to the sauce with the bacon. Press yolks through sieve. Put sauce on toast and then sprinkle with the yokes.

Recipe courtesy of Sandy Newton

Christmas Omelet
makes 24 servings

*C*hristmas Omlet is an old family tradition for Brion's family. His Dad had a giant restaurant pan made from heavy aluminum. The handle was so long we had to cut it partially off so it would fit in the oven. Even though that pan was passed on to Brion it was lost out of a van that we had stored for a long time. We miss the pan, but love and continue the tradition.

5 dozen large eggs

16 ounces of canned milk, approximate

1½ teaspoons salt, or to taste

2 to 2½ pounds sharp cheddar cheese

1. In a very large bowl crack all of the eggs, and beat until well beaten. Add canned milk and salt and mix well.

2. Preheat oven to 350 ° F and grease 3 9x13 inch pans.

3. Pour the egg mixture into the pans and then sprinkle the grated cheese on top. It will sink in but some will be melty on the top.

4. Bake in the preheated oven for 30 to 40 minutes, or until the omelet is very puffy and brown on top.

5. Remove carefully and serve hot with buttered toast and jam, and both original and maple-flavored sausage links.

Recipe courtesy of Deborah Robinson

Food for Thought

This recipe is straightforward and easy to adjust to any number of people. To determine how much to make I count the number of adults and children who are old enough to eat. I use 3 large eggs per adult and 2 per child. This Christmas I am planning on 16 adults and 8 children. The amounts in the recipe above are for that size of a crowd.

Ben's German Pancakes

makes 6 servings

E'ver since I was a teenager, I've been making German pancakes. I love the way they puff up in such a fun unique way. We love to eat them with syrup or powdered sugar, and whipped cream.

3 tablespoons butter

6 large eggs

1 cup all-purpose flour

1 cup milk

⅛ teaspoon salt

1. Preheat oven to 350° F.
2. Place butter in a 9 x 13 baking baking dish and place in oven as it preheats to melt the butter and warm the pan.
3. Crack eggs into a medium bowl and beat them lightly.
4. Add the remaining ingredients and mix to combine, but don't mix too much. Some lumps are fine.
5. By now the butter should be mostly melted. Remove the pan from the oven and carefully tilt it to get the butter to coat the bottom of the dish and part way up each side.
6. Pour the mixture into the baking dish.
7. Place pan in the oven, being sure there is clearance above the pan. The pancake will rise to sometimes double the height of the pan. Bake for 30 to 40 minutes, until golden brown.

Recipe courtesy of Ben Newton – adapted from www.allrecipes.com/recipe/36900

Food for Thought

In a convection oven, 30 minutes at 350 degrees works perfect.

Chefnotes

Some recipes recommend mixing the batter in a blender. I find this results in a batter that is too uniform, that doesn't rise as much or in as fun a way, and tends to be more dense.

If you prefer a more dense pancake you can multiply all ingredient amounts by 1.5, and use the same size pan, or use the same ingredient amounts in a smaller pan (9x9 or similar).

Christmas Morning Breakfast Ring

We have been making this breakfast ring every since our children were little. They have carried the tradition over to their families and Jenny's boys even request it for their birthday breakfasts.

22 frozen rolls (Rhodes rolls)

1 (3.5-ounce) package of cook and serve butterscotch pudding

½ cup melted butter

½ cup brown sugar

1 teaspoon cinnamon

1 cup chopped nuts, if desired

1. Grease a Bundt cake pan.
2. Place frozen rolls in cake pan and sprinkle 1/2 box of the pudding powder on top of the rolls.
3. In small bowl combine butter, brown sugar and cinnamon and pour the mixture evenly on top of the rolls.
4. Top with the remaining 1/2 of the pudding powder and the chopped nuts, if using.
5. Cover with a clean hand towel and let rise overnight.
6. In the morning, preheat oven to 350 ° F and remove the towel from the rolls. Cover them with tin foil in a tent shape so that the tin foil isn't touching the top of the rolls.
7. Place a cookie sheet in the oven on the lowest rack so that it can catch any drips.
8. Bake the breakfast ring, covered, at 350 ° F for 25 minutes. Remove the tin foil and bake another 5 minutes until the tops of the rolls are brown.

Recipe courtesy of Sherry Poulsen

Chefnotes

☞ I think using the whole box of pudding powder is a little too much so I usually only use about 2/3 of the box.

Burge's Brown Sugar Muffins

*T*his recipe came from Bryan's mom and has been a family favorite for a few generations. We make these for breakfast occasionally, but the majority of the time we make them as a compliment to our dinner. Yum!

½ cup (1 stick) butter

1 cup brown sugar

1 large egg

1 cup milk

2 cups all-purpose flour

1 teaspoon baking soda

½ teaspoon salt

½ cup walnuts (if desired)

1. Preheat oven to 350 ° F.
2. In a large bowl, cream together butter and brown sugar.
3. Mix in remaining ingredients.
4. Pour into greased muffin tins and bake for 15 minutes.

Recipe courtesy of Jen Burge

Sandy's Pumpkin Chocolate Chip Muffins

*M*y mom makes these muffins any time we are together. They are a bit gooey, but very tasty.

2 cups canned pumpkin

4 large eggs, beaten

1 cup applesauce

⅔ cup cold water

3½ cups all-purpose flour

2 teaspoons baking soda

3 cups white sugar

2 teaspoons cinnamon

1¾ teaspoons ground ginger

1 teaspoon nutmeg

1 teaspoon cloves

1 teaspoon salt

1½ cups chocolate chips

1. Preheat oven to 350 ° F. Grease muffin tins or loaf pans.
2. Mix all the wet ingredients together well. Mix all the dry ingredients together.
3. Combine the wet and dry ingredients and stir well.
4. Fold in the chocolate chips.
5. Pour into muffin tins.
6. Bake in preheated oven for about 20 to 30 minutes if using muffin tins or 50 to 60 minutes for loaf pans, until a toothpick inserted in the center comes out clean.
7. Allow to cool for 10 minutes before removing muffins or loaves from pans.

Recipe courtesy of Ben Newton – from Sandy Newton

Best of the Best Blueberry Muffins

makes 12 muffins

*M*ark loves the blueberries but there isn't always a muffin mix in the pantry.

½ cup unsalted butter

1¼ cups white sugar

½ teaspoon salt

2 large eggs

2 cups all-purpose flour, divided

2 teaspoons baking powder

½ cup buttermilk

1 pint fresh blueberries - rinsed, drained and patted dry

2 tablespoons white sugar

1. Position rack in the middle of oven. Preheat oven to 375 ° F. Spray the top of a muffin pan with non-stick coating, and line with paper liners.

2. In a large bowl, cream together the butter, 1 1/4 cups sugar and salt until light and fluffy. Beat in the eggs one at a time. Mix together 1 3/4 cup of the flour and baking powder. Beat in the flour mixture alternately with the buttermilk, mixing just until incorporated. Crush 1/4 of the blueberries, and stir into the batter. Mix the rest of the whole blueberries with the remaining 1/4 cup of the flour, and fold into the batter. Scoop into muffin cups. Sprinkle tops lightly with sugar.

3. Bake in preheated oven for 30 minutes, or until golden brown, and tops spring back when lightly tapped.

Recipe courtesy of Amy Trent – from www.allrecipes.com/recipe/40403

Mona's Pancakes

makes about 25 medium-sized pancakes   prep time: 5 minutes   cook time: 5 minutes   total time: 10 minutes

This is not an exact recipe because no one can make Mona's pancakes like Mona, but it sure does bring back some good memories!!!

2 cups all-purpose flour

¾ to 1 cup white sugar

1+ tablespoon baking powder

Dash of salt

1 large egg

⅓ cup vegetable oil

1½ to 2 cups milk

2 to 3 teaspoons vanilla extract

1 teaspoon almond extract, optional

1. In a large bowl mix flour, sugar, baking powder, and salt.

2. Whisk in egg, oil, milk, vanilla, and almond extract.

3. Butter or grease griddle and cook like normal pancakes.

4. They may cook faster because of all the sugar.

5. No need for syrup because they are so sweet. Just pop them in you mouth and enjoy!

Recipe courtesy of Stacy Schultz – inspired by Mona (Jean Poulsen)

Chefnotes

This is my version of Mona's pancakes. As we all know, she did not have a recipe. She just said "a little of this and a little of that." I did my best to watch her and make guesses about how much of everything she put in.

The almond extract is my addition, but it compliments mona's pancakes very well.

Mona's Pancakes

*M*ona made legendary pancakes! Her sweet pancake batter cooked into crispy (and sometimes a bit doughy) pancakes that didn't really need syrup. For Mona cooking was an art, not a science. She rarely followed or wrote down a recipe. Many have tried to recreate her pancakes, and many have failed to get it just right. We found the following recipe for pancakes written in her handwriting. Perhaps this recipe will get us closer to her yummy concoction.

2 cups all-purpose flour
1 cup white sugar
½ tablespoon baking powder
1 teaspoon salt
1½ cups milk
2 large eggs
⅓ cup vegetable oil

1 teaspoon vanilla extract

1. In a large bowl mix together the flour, sugar, baking powder and salt.
2. Then add the milk, eggs, oil, and vanilla, and mix till just combined.
3. Cook on a griddle, flipping only once bubbles pop and form holes that stay open on the edge of the pancake.

Recipe courtesy of Sandy Newton – from Mona (Jean Poulsen)

Food for Thought

Mona would sometimes use sausage or bacon grease instead of oil in her pancakes. I believe she would generally cook the pancakes at a low temperature to keep them from burning and to get them crispy. Her pancake batter was also good when cooked into pancakes after ageing in the refrigerator for a day or two.

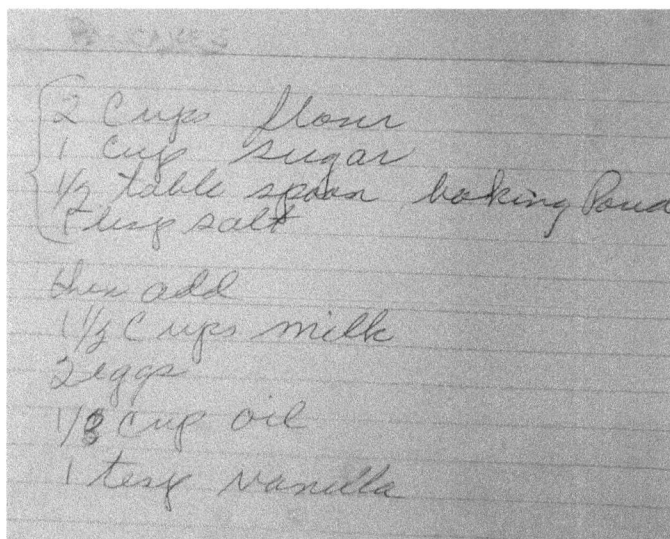

Sherry's Buttermilk Pancakes

2 cups all-purpose flour
1 teaspoon baking soda
1 teaspoon salt
2 tablespoons white sugar
2 large eggs
2 cups buttermilk
2 tablespoons vegetable oil or butter

1. In a large bowl mix all ingredients together.

2. Pour onto a preheated griddle or skillet.

3. Flip pancakes when bubbles appear on the edges and stay.

4. Remove when the other side of the pancake is golden brown.

Recipe courtesy of Sherry Poulsen

Corny Cakes

These sweet crumbly corn pancakes are quick and easy to make and have become one of my favorites. I love the crispy outsides, and the cornmeal texture inside.

1⅓ cups all-purpose flour
1 cup cornmeal
⅔ cup white sugar
2 tablespoons baking powder
1 teaspoon salt
2 large eggs
1¼ cup milk
½ cup coconut oil, melted

1. Preheat griddle to 350 ° F.
2. In a large bowl, mix together the dry ingredients.
3. Mix in eggs, milk, and melted coconut oil, until just combined.
4. Pour about 1/4 cup batter onto a preheated griddle or electric griddle to form each pancake.
5. Flip pancakes when they bubble around the edges.
6. Remove pancakes from the griddle once they are lightly browned.

Recipe courtesy of Ben Newton – adapted from Jiffy Mix Corn Pancakes

Chefnotes

Can substitute melted shortening or vegetable oil for coconut oil, but my need to adjust the amount (perhaps to be closer to 1/4 cup).
Wonderful with coconut syrup.

Sam's Favorite Pancakes

These are my favorite pancakes. I especially like them with berries and whipped cream.

1 ½ cups all-purpose flour

2 tablespoons white sugar

1 tablespoon baking powder

½ teaspoon salt

1 ¼ cups milk

1 large egg

4 tablespoons unsalted butter, melted, plus more for skillet

1 teaspoon vanilla extract

1. Whisk flour, sugar, baking powder, and the salt in a medium bowl.
2. Warm milk in the microwave until lukewarm, not hot.
3. Whisk milk, egg, melted butter, and vanilla extract until combined.
4. Heat a large skillet or griddle to medium heat.
5. Make a well in the center of the flour mixture, pour milk mixture into the well and use a fork to stir until you no longer see clumps of flour. It is okay if the batter has small lumps – don't over-mix the batter.
6. Lightly brush skillet with melted butter (optional if you have a non-stick pan). Spoon about 1/4 cup batter onto the skillet.
7. When edges look dry, and bubbles start to appear and pop on the top surfaces of the pancake, turn over. Once flipped, cook another couple of minutes or until lightly browned and cooked in the middle. Serve immediately with butter, syrup, and other desired toppings.

Recipe courtesy of Sam Newton – from www.inspiredtaste.net

Pumpkin Pancakes

When I'm pregnant I don't get to eat what I like. I missed a whole season of fall deliciousness once. To get even with the universe I spent some time looking for pumpkin recipes once I could hold down my food. I recommend eating them with cranberry sauce instead of jam.

1½ cups milk

1 cup pumpkin puree

1 large egg

2 tablespoons vegetable oil

2 tablespoons vinegar

2 cups all-purpose flour

3 tablespoons brown sugar

2 teaspoons baking powder

1 teaspoon baking soda

1 teaspoon ground allspice

1 teaspoon ground cinnamon

½ teaspoon ground ginger

½ teaspoon salt

1. In a bowl, mix together the milk, pumpkin, egg, oil and vinegar. Combine the flour, brown sugar, baking powder, baking soda, allspice, cinnamon, ginger and salt in a separate bowl. Stir into the pumpkin mixture just enough to combine.

2. Heat a lightly oiled griddle or frying pan over medium high heat. Pour or scoop the batter onto the griddle, using approximately 1/4 cup for each pancake. Brown on both sides and serve hot.

Recipe courtesy of Amy Trent – adapted from www.allrecipes.com/recipe/17036

Applesauce Oatmeal Pancakes

makes 8 servings   prep time: 5 minutes   cook time: 20 minutes

This recipe is adapted from the book "100 Days of Real Food; Fast and Fabulous" by Lisa Leake. I started making it when I was only eating whole foods and we have loved it ever since. I have changed some things like taking out butter, adding more applesauce and different kinds of fruit. The kids love it with blueberries, raspberries, or strawberries. I love it with apple slices in it as well.

2 cups whole wheat flour
1 cup rolled oats
4 teaspoons baking powder
2 teaspoons ground cinnamon
1 teaspoon salt
2 cups skim milk
1½ cups unsweetened applesauce
4 large eggs
¼ cup maple syrup or honey
1 apple, chopped into bite-sized pieces

(optional)

1. Combine all the dry ingredients in a large bowl.
2. Wisk all the wet ingredients together in a separate bowl.
3. Make a well in the center of the dry ingredients and pour the wet ingredients into it. Stir to combine.
4. Mix in fruit, if using.
5. Heat griddle or skillet to medium and pour about a cup of batter onto heated griddle. Flip when you start seeing bubbles on the surface and the underside is browned.

Recipe courtesy of Rose Frank – adapted from 100 Days of Real Food by Lisa Leake

Chefnotes

One cup of batter will make a plate-sized pancake that will likely be enough for a person's whole breakfast. This is how we do it, but feel free to use smaller portions of batter for smaller pancakes.

Ben's Fluffy Pancakes

makes 6 to 8 servings

*A*round the time our family was in Boston for a summer internship, we started using this recipe for pancakes. They are nice and fluffy, and rely on souring milk with vinegar for a buttermilk supplement, because who ever really keeps buttermilk in their refrigerator. I also tend to think that if a recipe calls for both baking soda and baking powder, it must be truly legit.

2 cups milk
4 tablespoons (¼ cup) white vinegar
2 cups all-purpose flour
4 tablespoons (¼ cup) white sugar
2 teaspoons baking powder
1 teaspoon baking soda
1 teaspoon salt
2 large eggs
4 tablespoons (½ stick) butter, melted

1. Combine milk with vinegar in a large bowl and set aside for 5 minutes to "sour".

2. Combine flour, sugar, baking powder, baking soda, and salt in a medium mixing bowl.

3. Whisk egg and melted butter into "soured" milk. Pour the flour mixture into the wet ingredients and whisk until lumps are gone, but don't mix too much.

4. Heat a large electric griddle, griddle, or skillet over medium heat or for electric griddle 275 ° F to 300 ° F. For pans that are not non-stick, coat with cooking spray. Pour 1/4 cupfuls of batter onto the skillet, and cook until bubbles appear on the surface. Flip with a spatula, and cook until browned on the other side.

Recipe courtesy of Ben Newton – adapted from www.allrecipes.com/recipe/162760

Food for Thought

Recipe can be easily halved, to make less.

Sherry's Maple Syrup

2 cups water

2 cups white sugar

2 tablespoons maple syrup extract

1 teaspoon vanilla extract

1. In a medium saucepan, combine water, sugar, and maple extract and bring to a boil.
2. Remove from heat and add in the vanilla.

Recipe courtesy of Sherry Poulsen

Blueberry Simple Syrup

*M*ark had blueberry bushes at their house growing up. We try to include blueberries in lots of our delicious meals.

1 cup blueberries

1 cup warm water

1 cup white sugar

1 teaspoon lemon juice

1. Mix blueberries, water, and sugar together using a whisk in a small saucepan over low heat until sugar is dissolved, about 5 minutes. Increase heat to medium and bring a gentle boil, stirring often, until syrup is thickened, about 15 minutes.
2. Whisk lemon juice into syrup; serve immediately or cool.

Recipe courtesy of Amy Trent – adapted from www.allrecipes.com/recipe/239712

Chefnotes

This recipe works well with other berries such as strawberries, raspberries, and blackberries. If using raspberries and blackberries, the seeds can be strained out for a smoother syrup.

Buttermilk Syrup

*O*ur family loves this syrup! I must admit, sometimes I just take a big spoonful of it and eat it by itself. Its delicious over pancakes, french toast, and waffles. Our favorite is to put it over my whole grain waffles.

1 cup butter
2 cups white sugar
1½ cup buttermilk
1 teaspoon baking soda
2 teaspoons vanilla extract

1. In a large saucepan melt butter, and add sugar and buttermilk. Bring to a boil.

2. After reaching a complete boil, boil for one minute.

3. Remove from the heat and whisk in soda and vanilla. Note: It will foam up during boiling and when baking soda is added.

Recipe courtesy of Jen Burge

Jen's Whole Grain Waffles

*T*hese waffles are very hearty and filling. I always make a few batches because we love the leftovers and I love to eat them plain as a snack. They are even better when served with whipped cream, berries and my buttermilk syrup (see page 34).

2 large eggs, beaten
1¾ cups milk
¼ cup canola oil
¼ cup applesauce
1 teaspoon vanilla extract
1 cup whole wheat flour
½ cup flaxseed meal
¼ cup wheat germ
¼ cup all-purpose flour

4 teaspoons baking powder
1 tablespoon white sugar
¼ teaspoon salt

1. In a large bowl whisk together the eggs, milk, oil, applesauce, and vanilla. Beat in the whole wheat flour, flax seed meal, wheat germ, white flour, baking powder, sugar, and salt until batter is smooth.

2. Preheat a waffle iron and coat with cooking spray. Pour batter into waffle iron in batches and cook until crisp and golden brown.

Recipe courtesy of Jen Burge

Sherry's Buttermilk Waffles

2 large egg whites
2 large egg yolks
1½ cups buttermilk
6 tablespoons (¾ stick) butter, melted
1½ cup all-purpose flour
1 tablespoon white sugar
1 teaspoon baking powder

½ teaspoon baking soda
½ teaspoon salt

1. Separate eggs, and beat egg whites till stiff, but not dry.
2. Mix remaining ingredients together, and then fold in egg whites.
3. Cook on a waffle iron.

Recipe courtesy of Sherry Poulsen

Dave's Waffles
makes enough for a family of 5

1⅔ cup all-purpose flour
½ teaspoon salt (or less)
1 tablespoon baking powder
2 large eggs, separated
1⅔ cups milk
¼ cup vegetable oil

1. In a large bowl, mix together dry ingredients. Separate eggs, leaving whites in a new medium-sized bowl, and adding yolks to the dry ingredients. Beat egg whites until peaks form. Add milk and oil to dry ingredients and yolks and mix to combine. Fold in egg whites.
2. Cook in a waffle iron.

Recipe courtesy of Stacy Schultz

Ben's Waffles

*S*omeday I'd like to write a children's book titled, The Awful Waffle Kefaffle, and in it I'll include the perfect Waffle recipe. I'm still hoping to perfect it more, but here is my current iteration. We eat waffles so often on Sunday mornings my kids say they are sick of them. My favorite way to eat waffles is with a small layer of peanut butter, sliced strawberries, real maple syrup, and topped with whipped cream. Waffles are really just an excuse to eat dessert for breakfast!

2 cups all-purpose flour or finely ground whole wheat flour.

2 tablespoons baking powder

3 tablespoons white sugar

½ teaspoon salt

3 large eggs, separated

2 cups milk

⅓ cup vegetable oil or melted coconut oil

1 teaspoon vanilla extract

1. In a large bowl whisk together the flour, baking powder, sugar, and salt. Form a well in the middle of the flour mixture.
2. Separate the egg whites form the egg yolks, dumping the whites into another medium bowl, and the egg yolks in the well in the flour mixture.
3. Beat the egg whites with a hand mixer until stiff peaks form. Set aside.
4. Begin pouring the milk into the flour mixture beating the egg yolks and milk together. Add the remaining milk while mixing the egg mixture into the flour mixture. Stir in the vegetable oil or melted coconut oil.
5. Preheat your waffle iron. Optionally, depending on your waffle iron, spray with non stick cooking spray.
6. Gently fold in the beaten egg whites.
7. Pour the batter onto the hot waffle iron, being careful not to pour too much (batter will rise substantially) Cook until steam is no longer visible.
8. Serve immediately with butter, syrup, peanut butter, nutella, powdered sugar whipped cream, jams, berries, or any other favorite toppings.

Recipe courtesy of Ben Newton – adapted from Dave Newton's Waffles

Chefnotes

🧑‍🍳 Can add 1 teaspoon cinnamon for cinnamon waffles, or add blueberries, chocolate chips, or even bacon to the waffle batter after poured on the waffle iron, but before closing it.
For faster preparation, and slightly less fluffy waffles, can add eggs without separating.

French Toast
makes 8 slices

*D*uring my mission, I received a small cookbook full of lots of simple tried-and-true recipes. It included this recipe for french toast. I assume it is nothing special compared to other French toast recipes, but I've used it for 20 years every time I make french toast.

French bread or other bread
4 large eggs
½ cup milk
1 tablespoon white sugar
Cinnamon, to taste
Nutmeg, to taste
Butter

1. Crack eggs into a medium or large bowl and beat. Mix in milk and sugar, then sprinkle with cinnamon and nutmeg and stir to combine.

2. Melt butter in frying pan or on griddle over medium heat. (optional for non-stick pans)

3. Dip slices of bread into egg mixture and fry until golden brown on both sides.

Recipe courtesy of Ben Newton – from the IDM cookbook and Zena Hunt

Baked French Toast
makes 6 to 8 servings

Suppose you were married to a person who loved to cook, and would get up early and make scrumptious things for everybody's birthdays. Now imagine that you wanted to make him something grand for his birthday breakfast...something he was not the king of making already...something that did not require you to wake up early and think. Here it is. Ta Da!

1 large loaf french bread, sliced

6 large eggs

2 cups milk

½ teaspoon nutmeg

1 teaspoon vanilla extract

1 cup brown sugar, divided

¼ cup (½ stick) butter

1 cup pecans, chopped

2 cups fresh or frozen blueberries.

1. Coat a 9x13-inch baking dish with cooking spray. Arrange the bread sliced in one layer in the baking dish.

2. In a large mixing bowl, add the eggs, milk, nutmeg, vanilla, and 3/4 cup of brown sugar, stirring well to mix.

3. Pour mixture evenly over the bread.

4. In a small saucepan over medium heat, melt the butter and the remaining 1/4 cup brown sugar, stirring well.

5. Top the egg mixture with pecans and blueberries, and drizzle with the melted butter and sugar mixture.

6. Cover and refrigerate overnight.

7. In the morning bake for 45 minutes until set and golden brown on top.

Recipe courtesy of Erin Newton – adapted from The One Armed Cook Book

Chefnotes

♟ Can use any kind of bread you want, including rolls or leftover bread.

Can replace blueberries with any kind of fruit desired: raspberries, peaches, etc.

Beverages

AH, DRINKS. Refreshment, hydration, time to sit and visit. In general, I think it best to eat your calories, not drink them. However, there are times when an appropriate beverage hits the spot both physically and emotionally, especially when it accompanies a friendly conversation. Catching up with cousins goes well with cold beverages. Although, these are often conversations that produce laughter and one should be very careful to not project the beverage out their nose... but, that is enough about that. Ahem.

Another more wholesome example... One long ago Fourth of July Ben and Big Amy and I made homemade lemonade for the last celebration of said holiday at Grandpa Robinson's home. We were in Grandpa's kitchen, the sun was shining, and I was expecting Libby. We used Grandpa's juicer to make the large batch of lemonade. Later, all manner of beloved family came and shared it with us as we reconnected. It was a rare and lovely day that I will always remember accompanied by a delicious beverage.

So, go ahead invite an old friend, or sibling, or cousin over. Prepare a lovely beverage. Welcome them in, sit somewhere comfortable and talk the day away.

Erin Newton

Emma's Delicious Orange Julius!

makes 4 to 6 servings   total time: 10 minutes

This is one of my favorite recipes to make because it taste so good. I made it for Mother's Day breakfast. Watch out for brain freezes.

1 (12-ounce) can orange juice concentrate
1 cup water
1 cup milk
⅓ cup white sugar
1 teaspoon vanilla extract

12 ice cubes

1. Put all ingredients in the blender and blend until ice is broken into tiny pieces.
2. Serve immediately.

Recipe courtesy of Emma Newton

Chefnotes

☞ Can add extra milk and/or ice cubes for a less strong orange flavor.

Homemade Root Beer

makes 64 servings

What summer picnic is complete without homemade root beer? It is so fun to let the dry ice cool and carbonate the sweet drink, which has such a unique taste!

6 cups white sugar
3 ⅓ gallons cold water
1 (2-ounce bottle) root beer extract
4 pounds dry ice

1. In a large drink cooler, mix together the sugar and water, stirring to dissolve the sugar completely. Stir in the root beer extract.
2. Carefully place the dry ice into the cooler, and cover loosely with the lid. Do not secure the lid, as pressure may build up.
3. If you can, let the mixture brew for about an hour before serving.

Recipe courtesy of Ben Newton – from www.allrecipes.com/recipe/43309

Chefnotes

☞ You can often find root beer extract by the other liquid flavorings on the spice aisle.

Lemonade
makes 2 quarts or 8 servings

The 4th of July after we got married, Erin and I were in charge of making lemonade for her family party. I had never made fresh lemonade before, but we used this simple recipe, and it turned out wonderful.... and I've continued trying to make lemonade whenever the world hands me lemons.

1 cup fresh-squeezed lemon juice (about 4 large or 6 small lemons)

7 cups water

1 cup white sugar

1. Combine the lemon juice, water, and sugar in a pitcher or large container.
2. Stir until all the sugar is dissolved.
3. Slice two of the lemon rind halves into four pieces each, and mix in.

Recipe courtesy of Ben Newton – from recipes.calputer.com

Food for Thought

If not drinking right away, consider using only 4 1/2 cups water and 20 to 25 large ice cubes (or about 1.25 pounds of ice). Then, as it sits out and the ice melts, the lemonade won't get diluted by the ice, and will taste just right when the ice is melted.

Creamy Hot Chocolate
makes 2 quarts

We didn't have hot chocolate powder, so I found this on Allrecipes. It was pretty awesome but I need to find a way to make it in a smaller batch...

1 (14-ounce) can sweetened condensed milk

½ cup unsweetened cocoa

1½ teaspoons vanilla extract

⅛ teaspoon salt

6½ cups hot water

Miniature marshmallows, optional

1. **Saucepan:** In large saucepan over medium heat, combine sweetened condensed milk, cocoa, vanilla and salt; mix well. Slowly stir in water. Heat through, stirring occasionally. Do not boil.

2. **Microwave:** In 2-quart glass measure, combine all ingredients except marshmallows. Microwave on 100% power (HIGH) 8 to 10 minutes, stirring every 3 minutes.

3. Top with marshmallows, (optional). Store covered in refrigerator.

Recipe courtesy of Amy Trent – adapted from www.allrecipes.com/recipe/63969

Hot Juice

This sweet hot drink is a favorite of both the Newtons and Poulsens. Growing up, whenever we got sick, mom would make us Newtons "Hot Juice", originally known as "Russian Tea". The Poulsens also called it "Hot Stuff." The tasty warm liquid seemed to soothe sore throats, relieve congestion, and warm you from the inside. It's not clear whether it contains any real medicinal value, but it is so comforting that I still crave it whenever I get sick.

2 cups white sugar

6 cups water

2 cups orange juice (or ½ cup orange juice concentrate and 1½ cup water)

¾ cup lemon juice

1 teaspoon vanilla extract

1 teaspoon almond extract

1. In a large pot, combine the water and sugar and bring to a boil, stirring occasionally.

2. Mix in the orange juice, lemon juice, vanilla, and almond extract.

3. Serve hot or warm.

4. Can be stored in the refrigerator and reheated.

Recipe courtesy of Ben Newton and Sherry Poulsen – from Sandy Newton

Chefnotes

Great for sore throats!

Chapter 4

Breads

 ROWING UP, the most common type of bread in my home was sliced sandwich bread from the store, so all that I really ever knew about bread was how to spread butter and jam on toast. Then, I served my mission in Chile and discovered the wonderful world of bread. It is so much more than a filler at a restaurant, or just a container that holds whatever you're eating on a sandwich. Unfortunately, even though I became a passionate connoisseur of the many kinds of chilean bread, I didn't start baking until years after my time in Chile. At this time, I'm still a novice, so I tend to just use the same recipe over and over, but I have dreams of matching the ability of the bakers from my youth. Give me some time, and like a good dough, I'll rise with proof that bread is not incidental to the meal, but a pure delight therein!

I once volunteered to make dinner rolls for a family reunion. I took my one recipe, quadrupled it, then spent the night mixing, kneading, and proving the dough in several bowls and sheet pans scavenged from around my aunt's kitchen. The next day, after putting them in the oven, I noticed that about half of the hundred or so rolls were paler than the others, and realized to my horror that in mixing the dough among the different bowls I had forgotten to add butter to one half. My uncle told me to brush the butter on top of them, saying that if I didn't say anything then no one would notice. They were such a hit that my aunt told me that I was in charge of making the rolls from here on out. I've had more unfortunate stories as well. I once fried a doughnut-like chilean dessert into a burnt inedible mess, but I consider stories like that to be learning experiences.

Baking bread can be a little daunting for the uninitiated. It's not as simple as mixing it all together and popping it in the oven. Like I said above, I'm still a novice, but my advice is to not worry too much. I don't know all of the science behind the process, but I know how long to knead the dough, how long it will take to prove, and how enough butter will make most things taste just fine. In this book you'll find some recipes to get you started. I suggest, once you're comfortable with the techniques, you make your own recipe. Try different flours, different sweeteners, different shapes, and even try adding different spices and flavours to give your bread a kick. Experimenting with your baking on your family will leave a lasting legacy of delicious treats and hilarious stories.

Wilder Koeven

Wilder's Rosemary Quick Bread Biscuits

makes 11-15 biscuits - depending on how you cut the dough

A quick and easy recipe for a savory companion to any meal.

600 grams all-purpose flour

1 tablespoon baking powder

1 tablespoon garlic powder

1 tablespoon onion powder

1 tablespoon rosemary

1½ cups milk

4 tablespoons melted butter

1 large egg

1 cup shredded cheese of your choice, optional

1. Preheat oven to 350° F.

2. In a large bowl, whisk all dry ingredients until mixed. If using, add cheese and use your hands to make sure it is fully coated in the dry mixture. This will ensure the cheese is evenly distributed.

3. Whisk egg and milk together, add melted butter to dry ingredients with half the milk mixture. Mix until incorporated, then add the rest of the milk.

4. Knead lightly to form a stretchy dough being careful not to over knead. Over kneading will cause the bread to become tough and dense.

5. Roll out dough in a circle about 1/2- 3/4 inch thick, then cut out 2-2 1/2 inch circles and stab several holes into each circle with a fork. (I use a cup to cut out the circles.) Don't waste the dough that doesn't make it in the first cuts, just reroll and cut until all the dough is utilized.

6. Place biscuits on a baking sheet, and bake in preheated oven for 25 minutes, turning the pan around after 15 minutes, until the biscuits are slightly brown on top.

Recipe courtesy of Wilder Koeven

Erin's Deluxe Biscuits
makes 12 big or 24 small biscuits

Sometimes I end up making up new recipes when I make mistakes or substitutions and like the result better than the original. The recipe just keeps evolving. Once, while making these biscuits, I used whipped cream instead of heavy cream. Everyone liked it so much, it became a new recipe.

3 cups all-purpose flour

4 teaspoons baking powder

1 tablespoon white sugar

1 teaspoon salt

¾ teaspoon cream of tartar, optional

¾ cups butter (or ½ cup butter and ¼ cup shortening)

1 cup milk (or 1¼ cup of buttermilk)

1 cup of whipped cream (not whipping cream)

1. Preheat oven to 450 ° F.

2. In a large bowl, stir together the flour, baking powder, sugar, salt, and cream of tartar, if using.

3. Make a well and cut in the butter with a pastry cutter.

4. Add the whipped cream and milk and stir together with a fork until it is all moistened.

5. Drop dough by spoonfuls onto a (greased) cookie sheet.

6. Bake in preheated oven for 10 to 12 minutes until they are golden brown. Best served immediately.

Recipe courtesy of Erin Newton – adapted from the Better Homes and Gardens Cookbook

Food for Thought

Feel free to experiment further. We like to add garlic, cheese or both. We have also added cinnamon and sugar for a sweet biscuit or added a little sugar and used them for strawberry shortcake.

Chefnotes

These biscuits are excellent with soup. May I suggest the split pea soup in this book (see page 87). I never add cream of tartar anymore. It seems to make no discernible difference. What is its purpose?

Flaky Buttermilk Biscuits

makes 8 to 10 3-inch biscuits   prep time: 20 minutes   cook time: 15 minutes   total time: 35 minutes

This is a biscuit recipe that I have only recently started using. It helped me understand how important it is to not overwork the dough, and how to get biscuits that have beautiful flaky layers, and a perfect golden crust. I love to make these with the kids helping, and allow them to cut them out, sometimes even using cookie cutters for biscuits of all sorts of fun shapes. Enjoy!

2½ cups (313g) all-purpose flour, plus extra for hands and work surface

2 tablespoons aluminum-free baking powder (yes, Tablespoons)

1 teaspoon salt

½ cup (1 stick; 115g) unsalted butter, cubed and very cold

1 cup + 2 tablespoons (270ml) cold buttermilk, divided

2 teaspoons honey

1. Preheat oven to 425 ° F.

2. Place the flour, baking powder, and salt together in a large bowl or in a large food processor. Whisk or pulse until combined. Add the cubed butter and cut into the dry ingredients with a pastry cutter or by pulsing several times in the processor. Cut/pulse until coarse crumbs form. If using a food processor, now pour the mixture into a large bowl.

3. Make a well in the center of the mixture. Pour 1 cup (240ml) buttermilk and drizzle honey on top. Fold everything together with a large spoon or rubber spatula until it begins to come together. Do not overwork the dough. The dough will be shaggy and crumbly with some wet spots.

4. Pour the dough and any dough crumbles onto a floured work surface and gently bring together with generously floured hands. The dough will become sticky as you bring it together. Have extra flour nearby and use it often to flour your hands and work surface in this step. Using floured hands or a floured rolling pin, flatten into a 3/4 inch thick rectangle as best you can. Fold one side into the center, then the other side. Turn the dough horizontally. Gently flatten into a 3/4 inch thick rectangle again. Repeat the folding again. Turn the dough horizontally one more time. Gently flatten into a 3/4 inch thick rectangle. Repeat the folding one last time. Flatten into the final 3/4 inch thick rectangle.

5. Cut into circles with a biscuit cutter, or into shapes with cookie cutters. Re-roll scraps until all the dough is used. Arrange close together on a baking sheet. Make sure the biscuits are touching.

6. Brush the tops with remaining buttermilk. Bake for 15 to 20 minutes or until tops are golden brown.

7. Cover leftovers tightly and store at room temperature or in the refrigerator for up to 5 days.

Recipe courtesy of Ben Newton – adapted from https://sallysbakingaddiction.com/flaky-buttermilk-biscuits/

Food for Thought

I suggest not twisting the biscuit cutter when pressing down into the dough. Doing so seals off the edges of the biscuit, preventing them from rising fully.

May want to line the baking sheet with parchment paper.

Macaroni Grill Herb Bread

makes 2 loaves

1½ teaspoons active dry yeast

1 cup lukewarm water

3 tablespoons olive oil

1½ teaspoons white sugar

1½ teaspoons salt

¼ teaspoon Italian seasoning

¼ teaspoon black pepper

¼ teaspoon garlic powder

1 tablespoon dried rosemary, crushed slightly

2½ cups all-purpose flour

1. Dissolve yeast in lukewarm water. Add remaining ingredients and mix to combine until a nice bread dough is formed.
2. Form into 2 loaves, and place on a lightly greased baking sheet.
3. Let rise 1 hour or more until double in size.
4. Bake at 350 ° F for 30 minutes.
5. Remove from oven and brush with olive oil. Let sit on rack for 15 minutes before serving.

Recipe courtesy of Jen Burge

Chefnotes

To eat this bread we break off pieces of it and dip them into an olive oil and balsamic vinegar mixture.

Ben's Oat Bread
makes 1 large loaf or two small loaves.

O ver the last 10 years I have perfected this recipe for oat bread. I make it in a bread maker, where it mixes, raises and cooks in under an hour. I love the smell of fresh baked bread, and this is such a simple way to achieve that. It is great to make in in the morning for breakfast, or with soup for dinner. When you are making the bread, be sure to remove some extra butter from the refrigerator. Once everyone smells the bread you'll need it soft and ready to spread on the warm slices.

1 ⅓ cups warm water (115-125 degrees F)

5 teaspoons yeast

2 tablespoons brown sugar

1 teaspoon salt

2 tablespoons butter

3 cups all-purpose flour

½ cup old fashioned oats

1. **Bread Machine Method:** Add all ingredients to bread machine, set to one hour 2 pound cycle (2 pound express), and press start.

2. **Manual Method:** Place warm water in large mixing bowl. Add yeast and stir. Stir in sugar and let proof (start to form a creamy foam) for 5 minutes.

3. Add salt, oil, flour and oats. Preheat oven to 200° F. Mix to form a ball then turn out onto a lightly floured surface. May need to add a bit of flour or water to get the dough just right (not too sticky but able to be worked). Knead by hand for 5 minutes (can use a mixer with dough hook for 5 minutes, if available). Place dough in an oven-safe oiled bowl.

4. Turn off oven, and place dough in in oven for 25 minutes until it doubles in size. Remove from oven and preheat oven to 350° F.

5. Spray two loaf pans with nonstick cooking spray.

6. With oiled hands, disturbing the dough as little as possible, divide dough and press gently into bread pans.

7. Bake at 350° F for 25 minutes or until golden.

8. Once bread is done, remove from oven and spread butter all over warm loaves. Let cool for several minutes before removing from pan.

Recipe courtesy of Ben Newton

Easy Homemade French Bread

*M*aking beautiful bread is actually easier than it seems. This recipe contains enough details that anyone can make two lovely loaves of french bread.

2 ¼ cups warm water

2 tablespoons white sugar

1 tablespoon active dry yeast

¾ tablespoon salt

2 tablespoons olive oil, canola oil, vegetable oil or avocado oil

5 ½ – 6 cups all-purpose flour or bread flour

1. In the bowl of an electric stand mixer fitted with the dough hook, combine the water sugar and yeast. Let the mixture bubble and foam before proceeding (this can take 3-5 minutes).

2. Add the salt, oil and 3 cups of flour and mix. Add in 2 1/2 to 3 more cups of flour gradually. The dough should clear the sides of the bowl and form a soft ball that doesn't leave a lot of dough residue on your fingers. Knead for 2-3 minutes until the dough is smooth. If the dough starts to cling to the sides of the bowl, add 1/4 cup of flour at a time until a sturdy but soft ball of dough forms.

3. **Rising Method 1:** Leave the dough in the mixer, cover with a lid or towel, and let the dough rest for 10 minutes. Stir it down by turning on the mixer for 10 seconds or so. Repeat the "rest and stir down" cycle five more times.

4. **Rising Method 2:** Instead of letting the dough rest for 10 minute spurts and then stirring it down, transfer the dough to a lightly greased bowl and cover with a towel or greased plastic wrap. Let the dough rise until doubled, about an hour or so, depending on the warmth of your kitchen.

5. Turn the dough onto a lightly greased surface and divide in half. Pat each section into a thick rectangle, of about 9X13-inches. Roll the dough up starting from the long edge, pressing out any air bubbles or seams with the heel of your hand, and pinch the edge to seal. Arrange seam side down on a large baking sheet lined with parchment paper (I use separate baking sheets for each loaf).

6. Slash several gashes in the top of the bread with a very sharp knife, bakers lame, or clean razor blade.

7. Cover with greased plastic wrap or a kitchen towel, and let the loaves rise until noticeably puffy and nearly doubled in size, about an hour.

8. Preheat the oven to 375 ° F and make sure an oven rack is in the center position.

9. Place the baking sheet in the hot oven and immediately toss 3 to 4 ice cubes on the bottom of the oven. This gives a delicious, classic, French bread crispness to the crust. Close the oven door quickly.

10. Bake for 25 to 30 minutes until golden and baked through, rotating baking pans halfway through cooking. Remove from the oven and, if desired, slather with melted butter

Recipe courtesy of Ben Newton – adapted from Mel's Kitchen Cafe

Ben's Bread Bowls
makes 8 to 12 bread bowls

*H*ow can you beat clam chowder in a bread bowl? Recently I started making bread bowls with this recipe, and it has quickly become a family favorite.

3 cups warm water

1½ tablespoons (2 packets) active dry yeast

2 tablespoons + ½ teaspoon granulated white sugar , divided

1 tablespoon salt

4 tablespoons (½ stick) butter , melted

7 to 9 cups all-purpose flour , divided

1 tablespoon milk

1 large egg white

1. In a small bowl, combine water, yeast, and ½ teaspoon of the sugar. Stir until the yeast is dissolved. Let stand until the mixture is foamy, about 5 minutes.

2. In a large bowl, mix together salt, 2 tablespoons sugar, butter, yeast mixture, and 3 ½ cups of the flour. Slowly keep adding more flour (about 1 cup at a time) until the dough starts to pull away from the sides of the bowl (I find that 7 1/2 cups flour total is about right).

3. Knead the dough (with a stand mixer, or by hand) for about 5 minutes. Stop and touch the dough with a clean, dry finger. The dough shouldn't be "sticky", but may barely stick to your finger. Add a little more flour, as needed, until you reach that consistency. Knead for 2 to 3 more minutes.

4. Lightly spray another large bowl with nonstick spray and transfer the dough to that bowl. Flip the dough over once so both sides are coated with the spray. Cover the bowl with a dish towel and let it rise until doubled, about 30 to 45 minutes.

5. Divide the dough into 12 equal pieces. Pick up one piece of the dough and pat it down with your hands to remove any big bubbles. Fold the edges of the flattened dough to the middle, then pick up and invert so that the seam is on the bottom. Gently stretch the outside of the dough ball stuffing the dough into the bottom, as you form a nice ball. Place the dough ball on one of two baking sheet lined with parchment paper. Using a sharp knife or razor blade, make an "X" on the top of each dough round.

6. Before you let the bread rise, beat an egg with 1 tablespoon of milk to make an egg wash. Lightly Brush the tops of each dough ball with a very thin layer of egg wash.

7. Cover the rolls really lightly with a piece of plastic wrap and allow to rise until doubled, about 30-40 more minutes.

8. Bake at 400 ° F for about 25 to 30 minutes. Allow to cool for at least 15 minutes before cutting for bread bowls. Make bowls by cutting on an angle around the top of the bread ball on an angle towards the middle of the bottom, being careful not to pierce the bottom. Then, pull off the top and pull out some of the bread from the center.

Recipe courtesy of Ben Newton – adapted from tastesbetterfromscratch.com/homemade-bread-bowls

Food for Thought

Can divide the dough into 8 pieces for larger bowls, but dividing into a dozen pieces seems to make bowls that are plenty big.

Sherry's Cornbread

½ cup butter, melted
⅔ cup white sugar
2 large eggs
1 cup buttermilk
½ teaspoon baking soda
1 cup yellow cornmeal
1 cup all-purpose flour

½ teaspoon salt

1. Preheat oven to 375 ° F.
2. In a large bowl mix melted butter and sugar.
3. Add the remaining ingredients and mix until combined.
4. Pour batter into a greased 9 x 9 pan.
5. Bake in preheated oven for 30 to 40 minutes.

Recipe courtesy of Sherry Poulsen

Bekah's Cornbread

1¼ cup all-purpose flour
¾ cup cornmeal
¼ cup white sugar
2 teaspoon baking powder
½ teaspoon salt
1 cup skim milk
¼ cup vegetable oil
2 egg whites or 1 large egg beaten

1. Preheat oven to 400 ° F and grease an 8 or 9 inch baking pan.
2. In a large bowl combine dry ingredients.
3. Stir in milk, oil and egg mixing just until dry ingredients are moist.
4. Pour batter into prepared pan.
5. Bake 20 to 25 minutes or until light brown and a toothpick comes out clean.

Recipe courtesy of Rebekah Emerson

James's Cornbread

1 cup cornmeal
1 cup all-purpose flour
2 tablespoons white sugar
1 tablespoon baking powder
1 teaspoon salt
⅓ cup vegetable oil or soft shortening
1 large egg
1 cup milk

1. Preheat oven to 400 ° F, and butter an 8-inch square pan.
2. Combine dry ingredients in a medium bowl and mix well.
3. Add vegetable oil or cut in the shortening until well blended.
4. Beat eggs and milk together.
5. Mix with dry ingredients until just blended.
6. Pour batter into buttered pan.
7. Bake for 25 minutes or until done.

Recipe courtesy of James Robinson

Chefnotes

☞ I usually use vegetable oil in this recipe, but the original recipe calls for shortening.

Erin's Sweet Cornbread

makes 12 servings   prep time: 10 minutes   cook time: 25 minutes   total time: 35 minutes

We love this sweet crumbly cornbread, and have messed it up in just about every way possible over the years. We've forgotten the salt, the egg, or the baking powder, or accidentally used baking soda instead of baking powder. Trust us, the recipe is best when you include all the ingredients.

1 cup all-purpose flour
1 cup yellow cornmeal
⅔ cup white sugar
1 teaspoon salt
3½ teaspoons baking powder
1 egg
1 cup milk
⅓ cup vegetable oil

1. Preheat oven to 400 ° F. Spray or lightly grease a 9 or 10-inch round cake pan or pie pan. (Double recipe for 9x13 baking dish)
2. In a large bowl, combine flour, cornmeal, sugar, salt, and baking powder. Stir in egg, milk and vegetable oil until well combined. Pour batter into prepared pan
3. Bake in preheated oven for 20 to 25 minutes or until a toothpick inserted into the center of the loaf comes out clean.

Recipe courtesy of Ben and Erin Newton – from All Recipes

Pizza Dough

makes 2 pizza crusts

1 tablespoon yeast

¼ cup warm water

3 cups all-purpose flour

1 teaspoon salt

1 tablespoon white sugar

1 cup milk

1. Dissolve yeast in warm water.
2. In a large bowl mix together flour, salt, sugar, milk, and prepared yeast.
3. Let dough rise.
4. Split dough in half and roll one half to form a round pizza crust.
5. Repeat for other half of dough.

Recipe courtesy of Sandy Newton

Food for Thought

This dough also makes good fry bread.

Naan

*A*t some point I got into a curry mood. You can only eat so much curry without eventually wishing for naan.

2¼ teaspoons active dry yeast (one package)

1 cup warm water

¼ cup white sugar

3 tablespoons milk

1 large egg, beaten

2 teaspoons salt

4 ½ cups bread flour

2 teaspoons minced garlic (Optional)

¼ cup butter, melted

1. In a large bowl, dissolve yeast in warm water. Let stand about 10 minutes, until frothy. Stir in sugar, milk, egg, salt, and enough flour to make a soft dough. Knead for 6 to 8 minutes on a lightly floured surface, or until smooth. Place dough in a well oiled bowl, cover with a damp cloth, and set aside to rise. Let it rise 1 hour, until the dough has doubled in volume.

2. Punch down dough, and knead in garlic. Pinch off small handfuls of dough about the size of a golf ball. Roll into balls, and place on a tray. Cover with a towel, and allow to rise until doubled in size, about 30 minutes.

3. During the second rising, preheat grill to high heat.

4. At grill side, roll one ball of dough out into a thin circle. Lightly oil grill. Place dough on grill, and cook for 2 to 3 minutes, or until puffy and lightly browned. Brush uncooked side with butter, and turn over. Brush cooked side with butter, and cook until browned, another 2 to 4 minutes. Remove from grill, and continue the process until all the naan has been prepared.

Recipe courtesy of Amy Trent – adapted from www.allrecipes.com/recipe/14565

Japanese Milk Bread Buns

makes 6 buns   prep time: 20 minutes   cook time: 4 to 5 hours

*A*nthony went through a phase where he made this recipe in some form every weekend. He has made it as hamburger buns, hot dog buns, rolls, and loaves of bread. You can form it in many different ways. Be prepared to devour one loaf right out of the oven with jam. It is like eating a cloud.

Tangzhong:

20 grams bread flour

27 grams water

60 grams whole milk

Dough:

120 grams whole milk

9 grams instant yeast

320 grams bread flour

1 teaspoon fine sea salt

2½ tablespoons (35g) granulated white sugar

1 whole egg

1 egg yolk

3 tablespoons (42g) unsalted butter, softened

Egg wash:

1 whole large egg

Splash of whole milk

1. **Tangzhong:** Whisk the Bread Flour, Water, and Whole Milk together until incorporated

2. Place over medium heat and whisk until the mixture thickens and becomes like a paste (25 to 30 seconds after coming up to heat)

3. Set the Tangzhong aside for now

4. Dough: Heat the Whole Milk to 95 ° F and add the instant yeast. Let that sit for 8 minutes.

5. Place the Bread Flour for the Dough in a stand mixer and add the sugar and salt. Whisk together until incorporated.

6. Setup your stand mixer with the Dough hook attachment and start on low speed. Add the Whole Milk mixture slowly.

7. Let that run for a few seconds and then add the Tangzhong mixture. Then add the Eggs and Egg Yolks. (Preferably these are room temperature.

8. Mix on medium low until reasonably incorporated (you may have to stop and scrape the sides occasionally)

9. Gradually add the butter while mixing at medium low speed.

10. Let that incorporate and mix for around 5 to 8 minutes or until that mixture is nice and smooth.

11. Lightly grease a medium size bowl.

12. Fold in the edges of your dough and place seam side down on a work surface and rub it around keeping constant contact with the surface to make a round shape and set it in the bowl.

13. Place a damp' towel over the bowl and place that bowl in a warm area for 1 to 1.5 hours or until it has doubled in size.

14. **Forming the Dough:** Once the Dough has doubled in size punch it down and put it on a work surface.

15. Using a bench scraper separate into portions per serving and weigh out accordingly (Each bun should be between 95 and 105 grams)

16. Gently fold the edges in and place seam side down and rub it around to make a round shape.

17. Once all the balls have been completed place them evenly spaced on a baking sheet lined with parchment paper. Should be about 2.5 inches apart.

18. Cover with another equally sized rim baking sheet to allow for rise and prevent them from drying out. (So one cookie sheet with another flipped over on top of it.

19. Allow them to rise for 1 to 2 hours or until doubled.

20. Brush the top of each bun with egg wash.
21. Bake at 375 ° F for 16 to 18 minutes or until golden brown on the top.

22. (Optional) Brush them with butter when they come out of the oven.
23. Let them cool on a wire rack.

Recipe courtesy of Anthony Frank – from Joshua Wiseman

Breadsticks

*T*hese are simple and easy and always a hit at our house.

1 tablespoon yeast
1½ cups water, divided
2 tablespoons white sugar
½ teaspoon salt
3½ to 4 cups all-purpose flour
6 tablespoons (¾ stick) of butter
Toppings:
Parmesan Cheese
Italian Seasoning
Garlic Salt

1. In a small bowl, dissolve yeast and sugar in 1/2 cup of lukewarm water, and set aside.

2. In a large bowl combine 3 cups of flour, 1 cup water, salt, and the yeast mixture.
3. Knead in the remaining flour, and cover for 10 minutes.
4. Melt butter and pour into a cookie sheet.
5. Roll out dough to about the size of the pan. Place dough in pan to coat one side with butter. Flip dough over, so the butter side is up, and sprinkle with desired amount of toppings.
6. Cut into slices using a pizza cutter.
7. Let rise until double in size, then bake at 350 ° F for 20 to 25 minutes.

Recipe courtesy of Jen Burge

Irish Soda Bread

*M*any traditional Irish foods aren't really eaten in Ireland today. During my two years there, for example, I only had corned beef once, and it was on a cold sandwich. Soda bread, however, I did have on my mission. Every year since Erin and I got married, I make a batch of soda bread for St. Patrick's day. I think it is best sliced and toasted.

4 cups all-purpose flour

4 tablespoons white sugar

1 teaspoon baking soda

1 tablespoon baking powder

½ teaspoon salt

½ cup butter, softened

1 cup buttermilk

1 large egg

¼ cup butter, melted

¼ cup buttermilk

1. Preheat oven to 375 ° F. Lightly grease a large baking sheet.

2. In a large bowl, mix together flour, sugar, baking soda, baking powder, salt and butter. Stir in 1 cup of buttermilk and egg. Turn dough out onto a lightly floured surface and knead slightly. Form dough into a round and place on prepared baking sheet. In a small bowl, combine 1/4 cup melted butter with 1/4 cup buttermilk; brush loaf with this mixture. Use a sharp knife to cut an 'X' into the top of the loaf.

3. Bake in preheated oven.

4. After about 15 minutes and 30 minutes of baking remove the bread from the oven and brush with butter mixture.

5. Bake until a toothpick inserted into the center of the loaf comes out clean, about 45 to 50 minutes total.

Recipe courtesy of Ben Newton – from www.allrecipes.com/recipe/16947

Chefnotes

You may divide the dough in half and make two smaller rounds, rather than one big one, if you prefer. The smaller rounds can both fit on a single baking sheet. Adjust the cooking time accordingly.

Mickey Mouse Rolls

*B*ecause of the three globs bread, which look like two ears, and a head, these rolls are called Mickey mouse rolls. I have no idea who first started calling them that, but they were "Mickey Mouse Rolls" as far back as I can remember. The recipe probably came from Grandma Bose.

2 yeast cakes dissolved in ¼ cup warm water

1 cup water

3 large eggs, beaten

½ cup white sugar

½ cup butter, melted

½ teaspoon salt

4½ cups all-purpose flour

1. Stir to dissolve yeast in 1/4 cup water, and set aside.

2. Mix to combine eggs, sugar, butter, salt, water, dissolved yeast, and flour.

3. Cover and let rise until double in size. Punch down and shape into walnut-sized balls.

4. Grease a muffin tin and place 3 dough balls in each hole.

5. Cover with a warm, wet towel and let rise.

6. Bake 12 to 15 minutes at 400 ° F.

Recipe courtesy of James Robinson

Chefnotes

Dough can be refrigerated. Let rise and stir down before refrigerating. Chill thoroughly. Allow to rise about 2 hours after shaping dough, and bake as usual.

Bread Machine Dinner Rolls

makes 16 rolls   prep time: 20 minutes   cook time: 20 minutes   total time: 2 hours and 20 minutes

When I don't have time to make refrigerator rolls, I make these rolls with the help of our bread maker.

½ cup warm water (110 degrees)

½ cup warm milk

1 large egg

⅓ cup (5⅓ tablespoons) butter, softened

⅓ cup white sugar

1 teaspoon salt

3¾ cups all-purpose flour

2¼ teaspoons (1 package) active dry yeast

¼ cup butter, softened

1. Place water, milk, egg, 1/3 cup butter, sugar, salt, flour and yeast in the pan of the bread machine. Select dough cycle or knead and first rise cycle and press start.

2. When cycle finishes, turn dough out onto a lightly floured surface. Divide dough in half. Roll each half into a 12 inch circle, spread 1/4 cup softened butter over entire round. Cut each circle into 8 wedges. Roll wedges starting at wide end; roll gently but tightly. Place point side down on ungreased cookie sheet. Cover with clean kitchen towel and put in a warm place, let rise 1 hour.

3. Preheat oven to 400 ° F.

4. Bake in preheated oven for 10 to 15 minutes, until golden.

Recipe courtesy of Ben Newton – adapted from www.allrecipes.com/recipe/17690

Marie's Refrigerator Rolls
makes 32 rolls

*F*luffy Crescent Rolls that are a highlight of every Newton and as of late many Robinson Thanksgiving meals and numerous Sunday dinners. Affectionately termed "Snail Cookies" by Matthew.

½ cup warm water
2¼ teaspoons active dry yeast
1 cup cold milk
¼ cup white sugar
1½ teaspoons salt
3 large eggs
5 cups all-purpose flour, divided
½ cup (1 stick) margarine or butter, melted

1. In a small bowl dissolve yeast in the warm water and let sit for a few minutes until frothy.

2. In a large bowl mix together milk, sugar, salt, and eggs.

3. Add the prepared yeast and half of the flour. Add margarine or butter and mix.

4. Add the remaining flour and finish mixing to form a sticky dough.

5. Transfer dough to a buttered bowl and refrigerate overnight or 8 hours.

6. Remove dough from refrigerator 2 1/2 hours before baking.

7. Using flour on your hands remove the dough from the bowl onto a floured work area. Divide the dough in half and roll out into a circle. Use a pizza cutter to cut the circle in half, and then in half again. Continue cutting slices in half until you have 16 slices (shaped like pizza slices).

8. Roll up each slice starting at the long end, finishing with the tail of the slice on the bottom of the roll. Then, bend each roll slightly and place on a greased baking sheet. Repeat for the other half of the dough. Prepared rolls should fit on 2 baking sheets.

9. Let rolls rise for 2 hours.

10. Bake at 350° F to 375° F for 10 to 15 minutes.

Recipe courtesy of Sandy Newton and Ben Newton – from Great Grandma Marie Newton

Jen's Amazing Potato Rolls
makes 3 dozen rolls

*M*y mom's aunt Marge is known for her amazing breads. Her potato rolls are probably her most famous bread! The secret ingredient is the potato flour because it makes the rolls so soft. When I was completing my college degree I had an internship in St. George and had the privilege of living with Marge and my Great Grandma Shurtliff. It was a very memorable time for me to spend so much time with my grandma and to help take care of her. It was also a great time to learn the tricks of the trade of bread making directly from the master herself. Marge didn't have a recipe, she knew it by heart and didn't need one. However, I couldn't go home without a recipe for these delicious rolls. So, every Sunday as we would make these rolls together, I was taking mental notes. After several weeks of roll making I was ready to write down the recipe. I measured out ingredients and wrote down the recipe in my own words, the way my brain thought of it. It has been a treasured recipe of mine ever since! My family is always excited when I make these rolls because they are simply the best!

3 cups milk

1 cup (2 sticks) butter

¾ cup lukewarm water

½ cup white sugar

3 tablespoons rapid rise yeast

6 large eggs

2 tablespoons potato flour

1 tablespoon salt

10-12 cups all-purpose flour, divided

½ cup (1 stick) butter, melted

1. Put the milk in a glass measuring cup or glass bowl. Cover the bowl with plastic wrap and microwave for 5 1/2 minutes to scald the milk. When done, add the butter to the milk, cover with the plastic wrap, and set aside to cool for an hour or more.

2. When milk/butter is cooled to lukewarm or room temperature, pour the milk into the mixer.

3. In a water bottle or dressing container with a pour spout, mix together the lukewarm water, sugar, and yeast. Set aside and let sit about 10 minutes.

4. To the milk mixture add and mix in the eggs, potato flour, salt, and 4 to 4 1/2 cups of flour (enough flour that it looks like a thick pancake batter). While the mixer is on, add in the yeast mixture and mix until creamy. Stop the mixer and cover with a lid or dish towel. Let rise for 20 minutes (set timer).

5. Turn mixer on and add enough flour so that the dough comes away from the sides, 6 to 8 cups. Mix the dough for 8 minutes on medium speed (set timer). Stop the mixer and cover with a lid or clean, damp dish towel. Let rise about 45 minutes or until dough is rising above the bowl.

6. Using latex free gloves, or bare hands, put hands in flour and then take a piece of dough, about a golf ball sized piece. Roll/pull the dough out a bit to lengthen it. Tie the dough into a knot and place on a cookie sheet. Repeat this step until you have formed all the dough into rolls. Let them rise for about 20 minutes.

7. Bake rolls at 400 ° F for 10 to 12 minutes or until golden brown.

8. Brush tops with melted butter as soon as they come out of the oven.

Chefnotes

☞ You have to have the potato flour or this recipe will not work. I use Red Mill brand and find it in the baking section of the grocery store.

I know the recipe may sound complicated but it's just the way I wrote it down and I promise it really isn't complicated at all. It just takes a little time.

I promise, you will love this recipe!

Grandma's Rich Rolls

1 cup milk, scalded

⅓ cup butter or shortening

½ cup white sugar

1½ teaspoons salt

4½ teaspoons yeast (2 packages)

¼ cup water, lukewarm

5 cups all-purpose flour, sifted

2 large eggs, beaten

1. Combine scalded milk, shortening, sugar and salt; cool to lukewarm.

2. Dissolve yeast in lukewarm water; stir and combine with cooled milk mixture; add about half the flour; add the beaten eggs; beat well. Add enough of the remaining flour to make a soft dough; mix thoroughly.

3. Turn out on lightly floured board and knead about 10 minutes, or until smooth and satiny.

4. Place dough in a warm greased bowl; brush surface very lightly with melted shortening; cover and let rise in a warm place (80° F to 85° F) about 2 hours or until doubled in bulk. Turn out onto a floured surface and shape into rolls.

5. Place on a greased baking sheet; cover and let rise 30 to 45 minutes or until doubled in bulk.

6. Brush with milk, melted shortening, diluted egg white or diluted egg yolk.

7. Bake at 375° F for 15 to 20 minutes.

Recipe courtesy of Deborah Robinson

Chapter 5

Soups

SOUP WARMS THE SOUL, puts a smile on your face, and brings families together. Memories of holidays and family seem to often be connected to food, especially soups. When I think of soups, I imagine Halloween nights with chili and cornbread, crowded church chili cookoffs, cold wintry nights, and Christmas Eve parties. Every Christmas Eve (or Eve Eve), our extended family gets together to celebrate Christmas. As long as I can remember, our tradition has been to have soups for dinner that night. We started with clam chowder, then added broccoli chowder (for those that didn't like clams), and then other new soups over the years. It has changed over time, but the tradition is still alive today. I am grateful to have such fond memories of my family that I can revisit in my mind every time I spoon that warm, liquidy goodness into my mouth.

Stacy Schultz

Beef and Barley Soup

1½ pounds stew beef
1 to 2 pounds soup bones
Salt and black pepper to taste
1 bay leaf (optional)
½ cup parsley (optional)
3 quarts (12 cups) water
¾ cup barley
2 cups carrots, cut up
¾ cup chopped celery

1 cup chopped onions
Pinch of fresh basil, thyme, or garlic

1. Dice meat and sauté in a large pot until browned.
2. Add bones, salt, pepper, bay leaf, parsley and water.
3. Simmer (do not boil) for 1 hour.
4. Add barley and simmer 1 more hour.
5. Add the remaining ingredients and simmer for 45 minutes over very low heat.

Recipe courtesy of Sandy Newton

Chefnotes

☞ Can just use leftover roast instead of stew beef and soup bones

Beef Stew

2 pounds beef stew meat, cubed
3 tablespoons vegetable oil
4 cubes beef bouillon
4 cups water
1 teaspoon dried rosemary
1 teaspoon dried parsley
½ teaspoon marjoram
½ teaspoon black pepper
3 large potatoes, peeled and cubed
4 carrots, cut into 1 inch pieces
4 stalks celery, cut into 1 inch pieces

1 large onion, chopped
2 teaspoons cornstarch
2 teaspoons cold water

1. In a large pot or dutch oven, cook beef in oil over medium heat until brown. Dissolve bouillon in water and pour into pot. Stir in rosemary, parsley and pepper. Bring to a boil, then reduce heat. Cover and simmer for 1 hour.
2. Stir potatoes, carrots, celery, and onion into the pot. Dissolve cornstarch in 2 teaspoons cold water and stir into stew. Cover and simmer for 1 additional hour.

Recipe courtesy of Jen Burge

Stacy's Chili

makes 6 to 8 servings

1 pound ground beef

1 (1.25-ounce) package of chili seasoning

1 (15.5-ounce) can kidney beans

1 (14.5-ounce) can diced tomatoes

½ to 1 (12-ounce) package frozen corn

½ cup water

1. Cook and drain the ground beef

2. Combine all the ingredients and let simmer for about 10 minutes.

Recipe courtesy of Stacy Schultz

Food for Thought

Great with cornbread!

White Bean Chicken Chili

1 medium onion, chopped

1 tablespoon vegetable oil

2 (14.5-ounce) cans corn, with juices

4 (15.5-ounce) cans great northern beans, with juices

3 cups chicken broth

2 (4-ounce) cans green chiles

1 tablespoon garlic powder

1 tablespoon oregano

2 tablespoons cumin

½ teaspoon cayenne pepper

3 to 4 cups fully cooked, canned chicken

1 (16-ounce) carton sour cream

1. Saute onion with oil in stock pot until onion is translucent.

2. Add in all the remaining ingredients except for the sour cream.

3. Simmer for 20 to 30 minutes.

4. Add sour cream right before serving.

Recipe courtesy of Jen Burge

Cheesy Vegetable Chowder

2 tablespoons butter

½ cup onion, chopped

1 cup matchstick carrots

2 stalks celery, chopped

½ tablespoon garlic, minced

6 cups chicken broth

3 large potatoes

1 tablespoon all-purpose flour

½ cup water

1 cup milk

2 cups broccoli

1 cup cauliflower

2 heaping cups shredded sharp cheddar cheese

1. Melt the butter in a large stock pot. Add the onions, carrots and celery and saute over medium heat until tender.
2. Add the garlic and cook for an additional 1 or 2 minutes.
3. Add chicken broth and potatoes and bring to a boil and cook until the potatoes are just barely tender.
4. Mix flour with water and when smooth add to the soup. Simmer until slightly thickened.
5. Add milk, broccoli and cauliflower and cook until vegetables are heated through.
6. Stir in cheese and allow to melt, then serve.

Recipe courtesy of Jen Burge

Sandy's Clam Chowder

*W*hen Dave and I got married there was a famous seafood restaurant in the valley called Bratten's They had amazing Clam Chowder. I can't remember how I got the recipe but it is the best Clam Chowder I have ever tasted. I make this at our family Christmas Eve party every year.

1 cup (about 1 medium) onion, chopped
1 cup (about 3 stalks) celery, chopped
2 cups russet or red potatoes, chopped
2 (6.5-ounce) cans minced clams with juice
2 cups water
¾ cup (1½ sticks) butter or margarine
¾ cup all-purpose flour
1 quart (4 cups) half and half or 1 cup heavy whipping cream and 3 cups milk
1½ teaspoons salt
½ teaspoon black pepper
2 tablespoons red wine vinegar

1. In a medium pot combine onion, celery, potatoes. Add the juice from the cans of clams and then add water to just cover the vegetables.
2. Cook until vegetables are tender, about 10 to 15 minutes.
3. Meanwhile, in a large pot, melt butter then whisk in flour until smooth. Allow it to bubble for at least 1 minute while mixing.
4. Add half and half (or cream and milk) a little at a time while whisking until smooth after each addition.
5. Add salt and pepper to cream sauce and mix to combine.
6. Add undrained vegetables and clams to the cream sauce and mix in.
7. Just before serving stir in the red wine vinegar to the chowder.

Recipe courtesy of Sandy Newton

Chefnotes

Stacy prefers to call this Broccoli Chowder and replaces the clams with 2 cups of broccoli. Consider serving in bread bowls (see page 59).

Ham and Potato Soup

makes 8 servings   prep time: 20 minutes   cook time: 25 minutes   total time: 45 minutes

This has been a favorite of mine, ever since I made it for dinner and Erin said it was "the best soup of this kind I've ever tasted." Still not sure if it tasted good just because she didn't have to make it.

3 ½ cups potatoes, peeled and diced

⅓ cup celery, diced

⅓ cup onion, finely chopped

¾ cup cooked ham, diced

3 ¼ cups water

3 12-gram chicken bouillon cubes or 1.5 tablespoons better than bouillon

½ teaspoon salt, or to taste

¾ teaspoon ground white or black pepper, or to taste

5 tablespoons butter

5 tablespoons all-purpose flour

2 cups milk

1. Combine the potatoes, celery, onion, ham and water in a stockpot. Bring to a boil, then cook over medium heat until potatoes are tender, about 10 to 15 minutes. Stir in the chicken bouillon, salt, and pepper.

2. In a separate saucepan, melt butter over medium-low heat. Whisk in flour with a fork, and cook, stirring constantly until thick, about 1 minute. Slowly stir in milk as not to allow lumps to form until all of the milk has been added. Continue stirring over medium-low heat until thick, about 4 to 5 minutes.

3. Stir the milk mixture into the stockpot, and cook soup until heated through. Serve immediately.

Recipe courtesy of Ben Newton – from www.allrecipes.com/recipe/56927

Italian Sausage and Tortellini Soup

1 pound mild Italian sausage

½ cup onion, chopped

½ cup green pepper, chopped

½ cup celery, chopped

1 clove garlic, minced

2 (14-ounce) cans Italian-style stewed tomatoes

3 cups beef broth

½ tablespoon Italian seasoning

½ tablespoon chopped parsley

½ to¾ pound pre-cooked, frozen cheese tortellini

1. Brown the sausage in a stock pot and drain fat once cooked.

2. Add the onion, green pepper, celery and garlic and saute for about 5 minutes until onion is cooked.

3. Add the tomatoes, beef broth, Italian seasoning and parsley and simmer for 15 minutes.

4. Add the frozen tortellini and simmer for 15 minutes or until the tortellini is heated through.

5. Can be served with grated parmesan cheese.

Recipe courtesy of Jen Burge

Tuscan Soup

makes 4 servings

*M*ark and I had a trend of going to Olive Garden. This is a good copycat recipe.

6 cups chicken broth

1 onion, chopped

3 (3.5-ounce) links spicy Italian sausage

3 large potatoes, cubed

1 bunch fresh spinach, washed and chopped

¼ cup evaporated milk

Salt, to taste

Ground black pepper, to taste

1. Remove skin from sausage and crumble into frying pan. Add chopped onion, and cook over medium heat until meat is no longer pink. If you are trying to cut fat, remove meat from pan, place in a colander, and rinse under cold water.

2. Place meat in a large pot; add stock and potatoes. Boil until potato is cooked.

3. Add spinach. Continue boiling until spinach is lightly cooked.

4. Remove soup from heat, stir in evaporated milk, and season to taste. Do not add any salt if using canned stock.

Recipe courtesy of Amy Trent – from www.allrecipes.com/recipe/12918

Chicken and Gnocchi Soup

*M*ark and I went through a phase where we went to the Olive Garden a lot. Eventually we got into a pattern of ordering soup and breadsticks. Then we decided to figure out how to make the soup ourselves. Thank you AllRecipes.

1 tablespoon olive oil
1 small onion, diced
3 stalks celery, diced
3 cloves garlic, minced
2 carrots, shredded
1 pound cooked, cubed chicken breast
4 cups chicken broth
1 (16-ounce) package mini potato gnocchi
1 (6-ounce) bag baby spinach leaves
1 tablespoon cornstarch (optional)
2 tablespoons cold water (optional)
2 cups half-and-half cream
Salt and ground black pepper to taste

1. Heat olive oil in a large pot over medium heat. Cook onion, celery, garlic, and carrots in the hot oil until onion is translucent, about 5 minutes. Stir in cubed chicken and chicken broth; bring to a simmer.

2. Stir gnocchi into the simmering soup and cook until they begin to float, 3 to 4 minutes. Stir in spinach; cook until wilted, about 3 additional minutes.

3. Whisk cornstarch into cold water until smooth. Stir cornstarch mixture and half-and-half into simmering soup. Cook until soup thickens slightly, about 5 minutes. Season to taste with salt and black pepper.

Recipe courtesy of Amy Trent – adapted from www.allrecipes.com/recipe/218794

Chicken and Wild Rice Soup

makes 6 servings

¾ cup dry wild rice, cooked
1 tablespoon vegetable oil
2 boneless, skinless chicken breasts, chopped
8 ounces fresh mushrooms
1 medium onion, chopped
2 garlic cloves, minced
4 cups chicken broth
½ teaspoon dried crushed tarragon
¼ teaspoon dried crushed thyme
⅛ teaspoon black pepper
1 (12-ounce) can evaporated milk
2 tablespoons cornstarch

1. Make sure to precook the wild rice as it takes about 50 minutes to cook.

2. Heat oil in a stock pot over medium high heat. Add chicken, onions and garlic and cook until chicken is cooked through. Add mushrooms and saute for a few minutes until cooked.

3. Add cooked wild rice, broth, tarragon, thyme and pepper. Bring to a simmer.

4. Combine a small amount of evaporated milk with the cornstarch in a small bowl or cup. Stir until smooth. Add to pot with remaining evaporated milk.

5. Cook, stirring occasionally, for about 3 to 5 minutes or until soup is thickened.

Recipe courtesy of Jen Burge

Creamed Vegetable Soup

makes 6 servings

*M*y family used to call this "Restaurant Soup" because it had been served at a restaurant and the family liked it so much they got this recipe.

1½ tablespoons butter
2 slices chopped onion (about 3-4 tablespoons)
1½ tablespoons all-purpose flour
3 cups milk
¾ teaspoon salt
Black pepper, to taste

1 can vegetable soup
½ cup grated cheese

1. Melt butter and cook chopped onion until tender. Add flour and blend, then add milk and cook stirring until smooth and thick. Add salt and pepper and cook 10 minutes. Add vegetable soup and cheese. Heat through and serve.

Recipe courtesy of Becky Robinson

Butternut Squash Soup

makes 6 servings   prep time: 25 minutes   cook time: 35 minutes   total time: 1 hour

6 tablespoons chopped onion

4 tablespoons margarine

6 cups peeled and cubed butternut squash

3 cups water

4 cubes (or 4 tablespoons granulated) chicken bouillon

½ teaspoon dried marjoram

¼ teaspoon ground black pepper

⅛ teaspoon ground cayenne pepper

2 (8-ounce) packages cream cheese

1. In a large saucepan, saute onions in margarine until tender. Add squash, water, bouillon, marjoram, black pepper and cayenne pepper. Bring to a boil; cook 20 minutes, or until squash is tender.

2. Puree squash and cream cheese in a blender or food processor in batches until smooth. Return to saucepan, and heat through. Do not allow to boil.

Recipe courtesy of Jen Burge – from www.allrecipes.com/recipe/12974

Chefnotes

Can use 3 to 4 cups of chicken broth instead of the water and bouillon cubes.

Erin's Split Pea Soup
makes 8 to 10 servings

I don't like peas. I have visceral feelings about them. My Dad and I sat beside each other at the family dinner table...probably because we were both left handed. He would always dish my peas up for me and I had to eat them all. Sad memories. "Erin, eat your peas." However, I really like super fresh uncooked peas picked right out of the garden. When I was little we would visit my Grandparents in Richland, Washington and pick peas from their garden. No cooking. They were delicious. When I attached myself to the Newton family I got to pick peas in their garden and enjoy them raw before they were blanched and frozen. .... But, I also really like split pea soup. Ben teases me because I dislike pease so much except for in these two ways.

8 slices of bacon

1 chopped onion

2 stalks of celery

3 carrots, peeled and diced

3 potatoes, peeled and cut, optional

3 sprigs of parsley

1 teaspoon thyme

1 teaspoon salt

Bay leaves

Ham, optional

1 pound of split peas

8 cups of boiling water

1. In a large pot, cook the bacon strips until crispy, then remove and set aside.
2. Sauté the onions and celery in the bacon drippings.
3. When they are sufficiently cooked, add the split peas and then the boiling water.
4. Mix in the carrots, potatoes, if using, and the parsley, thyme, salt, and optional bay leaves and ham.
5. Let simmer for about 4 hours.
6. Serve as-is, or mash or puree some or all of the soup, depending on your preference. I like to blend up part of the soup and add it back. I have used a blender, an immersion blender, or just a potato masher to blend the soup. However, it is also good chunky, without any blending.

Recipe courtesy of Erin Newton

Food for Thought

There are several ways to make this soup depending on how much time and effort you have to give and your personal preferences. The easy method, but not my preference, is to throw everything into the slow cooker except the slices of bacon. Cook in slow cooker on low for 8ish hours. Optionally, blend some or all of the soup as described above. Cook the slices of bacon until crispy, then break them up and add them just before serving, or as a garnish.

This soup is really good on a cold night with homemade biscuits (see page 54). Eat your peas!

French Onion Soup

makes 4 servings   prep time: 15 minutes   cook time: 1 hour   total time: 1 hour and 15 minutes

What could be better than cheesy bread on top of onion soup? I like to tease Erin because she ironically dislikes peas and onions in general, but her favorite soups are split pea and french onion.

4 tablespoons (½ stick) butter

1 teaspoon salt

2 large red onions, thinly sliced

2 large sweet onions, thinly sliced

6 cups (48 fluid ounces) chicken broth

1 (14-ounce) can beef broth

1 tablespoon Worcestershire sauce

2 sprigs fresh parsley

1 sprig fresh thyme leaves

1 bay leaf

1 tablespoon balsamic vinegar

Salt and freshly ground black pepper, to taste

4 thick slices French or Italian bread

8 slices Gruyere or Swiss cheese slices, room temperature

½ cup shredded Asiago or mozzarella cheese, room temperature

4 pinches paprika

1. Melt butter in a large pot over medium-high heat. Stir in salt, red onions and sweet onions. Cook 35 minutes, stirring frequently, until onions are caramelized and almost syrupy.

2. Mix chicken broth, beef broth, Worcestershire sauce into pot. Bundle the parsley, thyme, and bay leaf with twine and place in pot (could alternatively use smaller amounts of dry spices).

3. Simmer over medium heat for 20 minutes, stirring occasionally. Remove and discard the herbs. Reduce the heat to low, mix in vinegar and season with salt and pepper. Cover and keep over low heat to stay hot while you prepare the bread.

4. Preheat oven broiler. Arrange bread slices on a baking sheet and broil 3 minutes, turning once, until well toasted on both sides. Remove from heat; do not turn off broiler.

5. Arrange 4 large oven safe bowls or crocks on a rimmed baking sheet. Fill each bowl 2/3 full with hot soup. Top each bowl with 1 slice toasted bread, 2 slices Gruyere cheese and 1/4 of the Asiago or mozzarella cheese. Sprinkle a little bit of paprika over the top of each one.

6. Broil 5 minutes, or until bubbly and golden brown. As it softens, the cheese will cascade over the sides of the crock and form a beautifully melted crusty seal. Serve immediately!

Recipe courtesy of Ben Newton – adapted from www.allrecipes.com/recipe/91192

Chapter 6

Salads

I didn't have potatoes,
so I substituted rice.
Didn't have paprika,
so I used another spice.

I didn't have tomato sauce,
so I used tomato paste.
A whole can not a half can -
I don't believe in waste.

A friend gave me the recipe -
she said you couldn't beat it.
There must be something wrong with her,
I couldn't even eat it.

Author Unknown

THE BEST THING about salads is, no matter what you put in them they still taste good. Many salad recipes make a complete meal, resulting in a good and easy dinnertime. Enjoy your SALADS!!!

Sandy Newton

Charlene's Four Bean Salad

makes a good amount

1 cup vegetable or canola oil

1 cup vinegar

1 cup white sugar

1 tablespoon minced onion or ¾ cup diced onion

1 (14.5-ounce) can green beans (any style, but French cut works well)

1 (14.5-ounce) can cut wax beans (yellow/golden)

1 (15-ounce) can garbanzo beans

1 (15-ounce) can kidney beans

1. In a large saucepan, mix oil, vinegar, sugar and onions together. Stir over medium heat until boiling.

2. Drain cans of beans and add to the mixture. Bring to a boil.

3. Reduce heat to low and simmer for 30 minutes. Cool and chill, preferably overnight.

Recipe courtesy of Charlene Poulsen

Cafe Rio Creamy Tomatillo Dressing

1 packet ranch dressing mix

1 cup mayonnaise

1 cup milk

2 to 3 tomatillos, with husk removed

1 bunch cilantro

1 teaspoon garlic, minced

1 lime

1 jalapeño

1. Place all ingredients in a blender, and blend together until well combined.

Recipe courtesy of Stacy Schultz

Chefnotes

Remove the seeds from the jalapeño for a mild dressing.

Sarah's Salad

1 head iceberg lettuce

6 strips bacon, cooked drained and crumbled

1 (8-ounce) package frozen peas

½ teaspoon white sugar

½ teaspoon salt

¼ teaspoon black pepper

½ cup shredded Swiss cheese

⅔ cup green onions

½ to 1 cup mayonnaise

1. Tear iceberg lettuce into bite-sized pieces and place in a 9x13 baking dish.
2. Sprinkle bacon then peas, sugar, salt, pepper, cheese, and green onions over the lettuce in layers.
3. Spread the mayonnaise on top of the other ingredients so that it completely covers the top.
4. Cover with plastic wrap and refrigerate overnight.

Recipe courtesy of Sandy Newton

Ann's Spinach Salad

This recipe was submitted three times. It must be good. Charlene's family used to always request it for family parties.

Salad:

2 bunches of spinach, chopped

1 small head iceberg lettuce, chopped

½ pound mushrooms, sliced or chopped

½ pound Swiss cheese, shredded

1 pound bacon, cooked and crumbled

Dressing:

⅔ cup white vinegar

1½ cups vegetable oil

⅔ cup white sugar

⅛ to¼ cup onion, grated

1½ teaspoons salt, optional

1 to 2 teaspoons dry ground mustard

1. Chop the spinach and lettuce and place in a large bowl. In a large bowl mix together spinach, lettuce, mushrooms, cheese, and bacon.
2. To make the dressing, in a blender or small bowl combine the remaining ingredients and blend or mix until well combined.
3. Pour the dressing over the salad and toss to combine or serve dressing separate from the salad.

Recipe courtesy of Sandy Newton, Sherry Poulsen, and Charlene Poulsen – from Ann Summerville

Chefnotes

Sherry uses less onion in this recipe (1/8 cup).
Charlene uses less dried mustard (1 teaspoon), and leaves out the salt.
Sandy serves the dressing on the side, while Sherry adds it and tosses the salad.

Terri's Mandarin Orange Salad

*A*ny time the Newton's get together Terri brings this salad. She has a huge bowl that she mixes the salad up in and serves from. Stacy asked her for the recipe, and had to promise that she would never make it for a Newton party before Terri would give it to her.

½ cup sliced almonds

3 tablespoons white sugar

½ teaspoon salt

Dash of black pepper

⅛ cup vegetable oil

1 tablespoon parsley

2 tablespoons sugar

2 tablespoons seasoned rice vinegar

dash of Tabasco sauce

½ head iceberg or red leaf lettuce

½ head romaine lettuce

1 cup chopped celery

2 green onions

1 can mandarin oranges

1. In a small pan combine almonds and sugar, stirring continually.
2. Cook until golden brown, then immediately remove from heat and spread out on cake pan.
3. Let cool and then break up candied almonds.
4. To make the dressing, combine salt, pepper, oil, parsley, sugar, vinegar and Tabasco sauce, and set aside.
5. In a large bowl mix together both lettuces, celery, and green onions.
6. Just before serving add and mix to combine dressing, almonds and mandarin oranges with the lettuce mixture.

Recipe courtesy of Sandy Newton – from Terri Holt

Sandy's Wonton Salad

1 head iceberg lettuce

1 to 2 cups chicken, turkey, or tuna

½ cup sesame seeds

½ to 1 cup green onions

1 can water chestnuts

1 package wonton skins, fried

6 tablespoons white sugar

½ cup vegetable oil

3 teaspoons salt

6 teaspoons rice vinegar

1. In a large bowl mix together lettuce, meat, sesame seeds, green onions, water chestnuts, and wonton skins (may want to save some to eat on the side).
2. In a blender thoroughly mix remaining ingredients, and pour over salad just before serving, being sure to stir the dressing before pouring, if it has been sitting.

Recipe courtesy of Sandy Newton

Sherry's Wonton Salad

*B*oth Sandy and Sherry submitted Wonton Salad, but the recipes are different enough that I chose to keep them both.

1 small package wontons
Vegetable oil, for frying
1 large head iceberg lettuce, chopped
2-3 chicken breasts, cooked and cubed
1 (8-ounce) can sliced water chestnuts
2 green onions, chopped
½ cup sesame seeds
Dressing:
4 tablespoons white sugar
2 teaspoons salt
¼ cup vegetable oil

4 teaspoons rice vinegar

1. Cut the won tons into quarters and fry in hot vegetable oil. Once fried, place on paper towel. Set aside.

2. In large bowl combine lettuce, chicken, water chestnuts, green onions, and sesame seeds. Set aside.

3. In a small bowl combine dressing ingredients and mix well. Pour dressing over salad and stir to combine.

4. Add won tons to salad and serve.

Recipe courtesy of Sherry Poulsen

Chefnotes

🎩 Can serve wontons on the side instead of adding them into the salad.

Bowtie Pasta Salad

2 cups mayonnaise
2 cups coleslaw dressing
1 (12-ounce) package bowtie pasta, cooked and drained
6 cups cooked chicken, chunked
½ bunch of green onions, chopped
3 or 4 stocks celery, chopped
2 cans pineapple
3 to 4 apples

Grapes
½ cup slivered almonds

1. In a large bowl combine mayonnaise and coleslaw dressing.
2. Add cooked pasta and chicken, and stir to combine.
3. Refrigerate overnight.
4. The next day add remaining ingredients and mix well.

Recipe courtesy of Sandy Newton

Chapter 7

Vegetables

$\mathcal{H}$OW TO OPTIMALLY CUT AN ONION: I first became interested in the the problem of cutting onions in a way to make the slices as uniform as possible at a gathering with friends. One of my friends and colleagues, Dr. Gabe Feinberg, also a mathematician, pointed me to a YouTube video from Chef Kenji López-Alt. In the video, Chef Kenji López-Alt says he has a friend who is a mathematician, who claims that you should cut radially towards a point 60% of the radius below the center of the onion, and claims that this is related to the reciprocal of golden ratio, 0.61803398875...

I was intrigued by this, and even began cutting onions at home with this technique, just because it made me happy. Each time I cut an onion for dinner, my mind would wander. I would think about why this is true, and what techniques I could use to approach the problem. While this was meditative for me, these musings did not lead anywhere substantial over the span of two months. One day recently, my thoughts actually lead me towards a way to approach this problem. Within two days I had found the optimal way to cut an onion.

The goal of the optimization is to make the volume of each piece of onion as close to uniform as possible without having to move any part of the onion after it is cut in half. The idea is to cut the onion in half, then slice it perpendicularly to create the semicircular layers of the same width. For the finally cut, instead of slicing vertically (as I used to do) or radially towards the center, you should slice radially towards a point below the center of the onion. The depth you should aim for depends on the number of layers of the onion. For a one layer onion, you should cut towards the center of the onion. For two layers, you should cut slightly lower.

I found it mathematically interesting to think about what happens as the number of layers gets larger and larger (and hence each layer gets thinner and thinner). What I found, with about seven pages of work to back it up, is that you should cut to a point 55.7306692985664478851093059145927180832000302073...% of the radius of the onion below the center of the onion for an onion with infinitely many layers (and slightly closer to the center of the onion for onions with finitely many layers). I call this number the onion constant, and I denote this number with the Hebrew character samekh, because the character looks most like an onion.

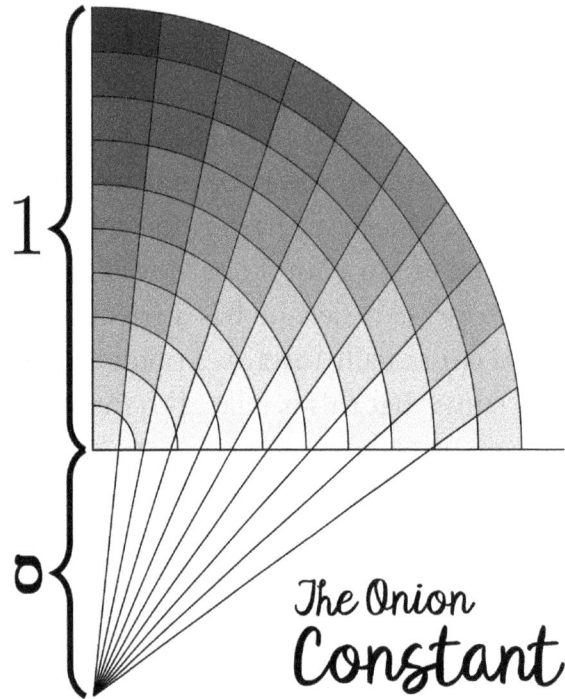

The Onion
Constant

I hope you all have a fun time cutting onions in an optimal way when you make the other recipes in this book!

Dylan Poulsen

Brion's Sunshine Carrots

Carrots
½ can frozen orange juice
¼ cup honey
2 tablespoons brown sugar
2 tablespoons butter
1 teaspoon cinnamon
Touch of cloves, optional

1. Peel carrots and cut in half and then cut into equal-size carrot sticks. Place in a microwave safe casserole dish (or container).

2. Boil carrots in the microwave until they start to soften.

3. In a small saucepan mix the remaining ingredients and heat until all items are mixed and fairly thick.

4. Pour sauce over the carrots and cook in the microwave until they are cooked through.

Recipe courtesy of Brion Robinson

Sandy's Sunshine Carrots

makes 4 servings

*A*lso known as "candy carrots," these sweet buttery orange-flavored carrots are one of my favorites, and are a hit with the kids as well.

5 medium carrots
1 tablespoons white sugar
1 teaspoon cornstarch
¼ teaspoon ground ginger
¼ teaspoon salt
¼ cup orange juice or⅛ cup orange juice concentrate and⅛ cup water
2 tablespoons butter or margarine

1. Cut carrots on the bias in about one inch chunks.
2. Cook covered in boiling salted water until just tender, about 20 minutes.
3. Drain water from carrots.
4. In a saucepan mix sugar, cornstarch, ginger, and salt.
5. Add juice and cook stirring until thick and bubbly.
6. Boil one minute.
7. Stir in butter, and toss with carrots

Recipe courtesy of Ben Newton – Sandy Newton

Milla's Ratatouille

*Y*ou know the movie with the rat who cooks? I watched the movie once and left with an intense desire for vegetables, as usual, but I didn't make it because I was trying desperately to do homework and sleep and work, etc. Then I moved to North Carolina and worked for a super fancy catering company where I tried lots of marvelous foods, and this was one of them. When I went back to school, I made it in desperation one weekend when I really needed vegetables. It's the ultimate comfort food. Eat by itself or over pasta. Use it to impress boys you really like.

Also- the traditional recipe includes red peppers. I think peppers ruin it, so I never use them.

All these amounts are really to taste- these are more guidelines than actual rules.

2-3 eggplants
4-5 yellow crookneck squashes
4-5 zucchinis
6-8 Roma tomatoes
1 (16-ounce) can of crushed tomatoes
2 yellow onions
6ish cloves of garlic, minced
1 to 2 tablespoons basil (see note)
1 cup olive oil, approximate
Salt and black pepper, to taste

1. Dice the onion and garlic. (Or take the garlic out of the freezer if you're lucky)
2. Add 1-2 tablespoons of olive oil to a large stockpot and heat on medium-high.
3. Add the onion and garlic to the stockpot.
4. Stir in salt, pepper, and a few teaspoons of dried basil.
5. While onions are sautéing, dice the other vegetables. Do not peel them first.
6. When onions are soft and translucent, begin adding eggplant, zucchini, and squash a few cups at a time. Don't add tomatoes yet.
7. Stir and add more olive oil as needed to keep everything coated.
8. Let the vegetables cook down slowly, adding more every few minutes as the added vegetables get softer.
9. Once you've added about half of the eggplant, squash, and zucchini, add the pureed tomatoes and the diced Roma tomatoes, then stir. (The liquid in the tomatoes will provide a base that will simmer. As you add the rest of the vegetables, they will simmer in liquid instead of sauté in oil, and you'll get a mixture of textures when you're done.)
10. Continue adding vegetables a few cups at a time. If it looks too much like spaghetti sauce, add a little olive oil, a few teaspoons at a time. Add more when the spirit moves you.
11. Once everything is added, let simmer on low heat for about half an hour, then serve.

Recipe courtesy of Amy Koeven

Food for Thought

This recipe freezes really well in gallon bags, so make big batches!

I recommend using frozen minced garlic and basil that is frozen, fresh, or blended, (but dried works too). If I have the option, I usually use a combination of blended and dried basil.

Can purée additional tomatoes yourself with salt and pepper and use in place of canned crushed tomatoes.

Chapter 8

Side Dishes

A COUPLE OF YEARS AGO, Erin and I found ourselves on a Friday evening in Santa Fe, New Mexico, looking for somewhere to eat dinner. Santa Fe has a lot of unique restaurants, so it was difficult to choose where to eat. We weren't in the mood for Mexican food, of which there is plenty in Santa Fe. We walked to a few restaurants only to find they had long waiting lists to get in. We were getting hungry by now, and finally, found a highly-rated restaurant that didn't look too busy. We decided to glance at the menu before going inside. One of the side dishes on their menu came with "edible dirt". I suspect we missed out on some of the best dirt in town, but needless to say we chose not to eat there, and after at least another 20 minutes of walking around, we finally settled on pizza. Never did check to see if that restaurant served mud pies.

Ben Newton

Newton Four Can Fruit Salad

*W*as there was ever a Newton summer family get together when this salad wasn't served? It's so sweet it definitely qualifies as a dessert, but its simplicity made it a staple.

1 (20-ounce) can pineapple chunks, with juice

1 (11-ounce) can mandarin oranges, drained

1 (15-ounce) can fruit cocktail, drained

1 (3.4-ounce) package instant lemon pudding

1. Pour canned fruit into a bowl, keeping pineapple juice, and draining other juices. Sprinkle pudding over the fruit and mix to combine.

Recipe courtesy of Ben Newton

Chefnotes

Can add coconut, bananas, marshmallows or yogurt for variety.
Can also be made with other pudding flavors, such as vanilla or coconut.

Raspberry Jello

3 (3-ounce) packages raspberry gelatin

2 cups boiling water

24-ounce package frozen raspberries

1 can crushed pineapple

1¾ cups cold water

1 cup sour cream

1 cup pecans, chopped

1. In medium mixing bowl dissolve gelatin in boiling water. Mix in raspberries, pineapple, and cold water.

2. Pour half of the mixture in a 9x13 pan and chill until set, about one hour.

3. Spread sour cream on top of the set gelatin and sprinkle the nuts over the sour cream. Pour the rest of the gelatin mixture on top and chill until set.

Recipe courtesy of Sherry Poulsen

Betty Robinson's Christmas Salad

makes about 12 to 15 servings

*B*etty would often bring this delicious salad to Robinson family holiday dinners. It is colorful and festive-looking with its three-layers and is very rich and tasty.

1 (3-ounce) package lime gelatin

1 (3-ounce) package lemon gelatin

1 (3-ounce) package raspberry gelatin

3 cups boiling water

1½ cups cold water

1 cup miniature marshmallows

6 ounces cream cheese, softened

½ cup mayonnaise

1 cup whipped cream, whipped

1 (16-ounce) can crushed pineapple

1. Dissolve each flavor of gelatin separately in 1 cup boiling water. Mix 3/4 cup cold water into each of the lime and raspberry gelatin. Pour the lime gelatin into a 9" x 13" pan and put it in fridge to soft-set. Keep raspberry gelatin at room temperature, and set aside. To the lemon gelatin add the softened cream cheese, mayonnaise, whipped cream (whipped), marshmallows, and pineapple. Chill lemon mixture until thickened, then pour over soft set lime gelatin. When both layers are soft set, add thickened raspberry gelatin. Chill until set.

Recipe courtesy of Becky Robinson – from Betty Robinson

Shalyce's Strawberry Pretzel & Cream Cheese Jello

A favorite of not just Shalyce's. So delicious, great with just about any family dinner or holiday dinner.

2 to 3 cups crushed pretzels

¾ cup butter, melted

3 tablespoons white sugar

1 (8 ounce) package cream cheese, softened

1 cup white sugar

1 (8 ounce) carton frozen whipped topping, thawed

2 (3 ounce) packages strawberry gelatin

2 cups boiling water

1½ cups cold water

2 (10 ounce) packages frozen strawberries

1. Preheat oven to 400°F
2. Stir together crushed pretzels, melted butter and 3 tablespoons white sugar; mix well and press mixture into bottom of 9x13-inch baking dish.
3. Bake 10 minutes until set; set aside to cool (DO NOT OVERBAKE!).
4. In a large mixing bowl cream together cream cheese and 1 cup white sugar.
5. Fold in whipped topping.
6. Spread mixture onto cooled crust (all the way to edges).
7. Dissolve gelatin in boiling water.
8. Stir in cold water and frozen strawberries and allow to set in fridge briefly (to about consistency of egg whites).
9. Pour and spread gelatin mixture over cream cheese layer.
10. Refrigerate until fully set.

Recipe courtesy of Jo Jacobs

Food for Thought

Can use less sugar, if desired.

Chefnotes

We like to use frozen raspberries and raspberry gelatin instead of strawberries. A combination of the two could also be used.

Milla's Rainbow Jello

When I was in the singles ward in North Carolina, we had a "break the fast" meal every fast Sunday, and they had themes. One particular theme was "Utah's finest foods." I made a 14-layer jello, and it was a great alternative to the many versions of funeral potatoes, Jello fluff, and Jello with shredded carrots. Not kidding.

6 (3-ounce) packages gelatin dessert of various colors and flavors

6 cups boiling water, divided

3 cups cold water, divided

2 cups sour cream or plain greek yogurt, divided

1. Into a glass measuring cup with a pouring edge, pour half of a 3-ounce package of gelatin mix. Add 1/2 cup boiling water and stir until gelatin is completely dissolved, about 2 minutes. Then, stir in 1/2 cup cold water.

2. Pour gelatin into a 9x13 glass dish. Place a dish towel on a level shelf in the refrigerator. Carefully place the glass dish on the dish towel in the refrigerator, ensuring there is enough room to easily pour more gelatin into the dish without removing it from the refrigerator.

3. Immediately prepare the next layer of gelatin. In the glass measuring cup, pour half a package of gelatin mix, add 1/2 cup boiling water, and stir to dissolve (about 2 minutes). For a translucent layer, stir in 1/2 cup cold water, or for an opaque layer, stir in 1/3 cup sour cream or greek yogurt and thoroughly whisk it while the gelatin is still hot, until totally smooth. Let gelatin cool at room-temperature for about 30 minutes, while the previous layer gets firm in the refrigerator.

4. Keeping the glass dish in the refrigerator, carefully pour the cooled gelatin over the previous layer. Don't pour in just one spot, which may cause the gelatin to break through to the previous layer. Instead, move the measuring cup as you pour.

5. Repeat the previous two steps, alternating between translucent and opaque layers until the dish is filled with beautiful thin layers of gelatin!

Recipe courtesy of Amy Koeven

Chefnotes

☞ Best to use a clear dish for obvious reasons, unless you want to surprise everyone! Use a glass measuring cup with a pouring edge so that you don't make a mess in the fridge. Always pour the layers with the dish in the fridge to keep them smooth. Invest in an electric kettle for your sanity. When making a many layered jello, the process is time consuming. Give yourself plenty of time, usually about a half hour per layer, or 6 hours for 12 layers. As soon as you pour in a layer, make the jello for the next layer, and leave it to cool on the counter while the fridge layer gets firm. This saves a lot of time because it will be so much cooler when you finally put it in the fridge, and you're less likely to break through the layer beneath. Scatter berries wherever the spirit moves you.

Potatoes Au Gratin

When Dave was a stake clerk they use to have a meal for visiting general authorities, between an afternoon leadership meeting and the night meeting on Saturday. President Butterfield's wife Marge brought this recipe to me to make for that dinner. It is the best recipe for funeral potatoes that I have ever tasted.

8 large potatoes

½ cup margarine

1 (10.5-ounce) can cream of chicken soup

⅓ cup green onions

1 pint (2 cups) sour cream

¾ cup grated cheese

1. In a large pot of boiling water, cook potatoes with skin on until tender.

2. Let potatoes cool, then peel and grate into a large bowl.

3. Preheat oven to 350 ° F.

4. In a saucepan heat margarine and soup together.

5. Add green onions, sour cream, and cheese and mix to combine.

6. Stir mixture into grated potatoes

7. Pour into a 9x13 baking dish and cook in preheated oven for about 30 minutes, until heated through.

Recipe courtesy of Sandy Newton

Cheesy Baked Potatoes on the Grill

makes 4 baked potatoes   prep time: 15 minutes   total time: 30 minutes

Suppose it's a hot day in the middle of the summer and you have a craving for a baked potato with your meal, but can't bear the thought of turning on the oven for an hour, and worse, dinner is in 30 minutes. Never fear. With this recipe you can get beautiful baked potatoes in under 30 minutes from your microwave and your barbecue grill, never needing to turn on your oven.

Potatoes:
4 medium baking or russet potatoes
1 tablespoon butter, melted or vegetable oil
½ teaspoon salt or seasoned salt

Topping:
¼ cup butter, softened
½ cup (about 2 ounces) cheese, shredded
2 tablespoons fresh parsley, chopped

Finishing Touch:
Garlic powder
Black pepper

1. Heat gas or charcoal grill.
2. Pierce potatoes with a fork to allow steam to escape. Brush or rub outside of potatoes with melted butter or vegetable oil; sprinkle with salt or seasoned salt, getting it on all sides of the potatoes.
3. Place potatoes on microwavable plate or in shallow microwavable dish. Microwave on High 6 to 8 minutes, turning once, until fork-tender.
4. Meanwhile, in a small bowl, mix the topping by blending together the softened butter, cheese and parsley.
5. Place potatoes on the grill over medium heat. Cover grill and cook 8 to 12 minutes, turning occasionally, until crisp and browned.
6. Remove from grill and cut a large X in the top of each baked potato; press sides slightly to fluff. Top each with the cheesy butter topping and sprinkle lightly with garlic powder and pepper (optional).

Recipe courtesy of Ben Newton – adapted from BettyCrocker.com

Chefnotes

Can use any cheese variety, but we often use a cheddar Monterey jack blend.
Can substitute 2 teaspoons dried parsley for fresh.

Erin's Coconut Rice and Beans

makes 4 to 6 servings

This recipe is much loved in our family and has undergone many changes. Don't be afraid to try variations.

2 cups uncooked rice

2½ cups water

1 (13.5-ounce) can coconut milk

½ tablespoon white sugar

1 (15.5-ounce) can red beans, drained and rinsed

Pinch of salt

1. Use any kind of rice that you like. Rinse and drain the rice. Our family has visited a rice processing factory. Let me tell you, you should always wash your rice. Meow ... need I say more?

2. Combine all ingredients in a rice cooker. Gently stir it all together and start the rice cooker.

3. If you're not a fan of a rice cooker: Bring to a boil over medium heat. Cover, reduce heat and simmer 18 to 20 minutes until rice is tender.

Recipe courtesy of Erin Newton

Food for Thought

My original notion for this recipe came from the rice served at Rumbi Island Grill.

Serve with smoked pork, carne asada, or chicken and a lovely mix of steamed vegetables, such as broccoli, celery, carrots and so forth.

We like to top with our own Asian sauce or Mr. Yoshida's Sweet Teriyaki Original Gourmet Sauce.

Chefnotes

Can substitute pink beans or black beans for red beans.

Any type of rice will work. We most often use Botan brand calrose rice or Nishiki short grain rice.

We often double or 1 1/2 this recipe and it works great. We find all kinds of uses for this rice. I hope you enjoy.

Crispy Baked Tofu

makes 4 servings   prep time: 15 minutes   cook time: 25 minutes

*A*nthony's mom came and had dinner with us one night. We had Thai curry and included this recipe for tofu. She has historically hated tofu so we also made chicken but she ended up liking this tofu. The kids think it is great and when I include these with Thai cabbage wraps, it is the only part they want to eat.

1 block (12 to 15 ounces) organic extra-firm tofu

1 tablespoon extra-virgin olive oil

1 tablespoon tamari or soy sauce

1 tablespoon cornstarch or arrowroot starch

1. Preheat the oven to 400° F and line a large, rimmed baking sheet with parchment paper to prevent the tofu from sticking.

2. **To prepare the tofu:** Drain the tofu and use your palms to gently squeeze out some of the water. Slice the tofu into thirds lengthwise so you have 3 even slabs. Stack the slabs on top of each other and slice through them lengthwise to make 3 even columns, then slice across to make 5 even rows.

3. Line a cutting board with a lint-free tea towel or paper towels, then arrange the tofu in an even layer on the towel(s). Fold the towel(s) over the cubed tofu, then place something heavy on top (like another cutting board, topped with a cast iron pan or large cans of tomatoes) to help the tofu drain. Let the tofu rest for at least 10 minutes (preferably more like 30 minutes, if you have the time).

4. Transfer the pressed tofu to a medium mixing bowl and drizzle with the olive oil and tamari. Toss to combine. Sprinkle the starch over the tofu, and toss the tofu until the starch is evenly coated, so there are no powdery spots remaining.

5. Tip the bowl of tofu over onto your prepared baking sheet and arrange the tofu in an even layer. Bake for 25 to 30 minutes, tossing the tofu halfway, until the tofu is deeply golden on the edges. Use as desired.

Recipe courtesy of Rose Frank – from Cookie and Kate

Chapter 9

Casseroles

RECENTLY I swapped all the labels on my wife's spices. She hasn't realized yet, but the thyme is cumin.

Broccoli & Chicken Casserole

2 (10-ounce) packages frozen, cooked, broccoli

2 cups cooked chicken, cubed

2 (10.5-ounce) cans cream of chicken soup

1 cup mayonnaise

½ teaspoon lemon juice

¾ teaspoon curry powder

1½ cups grated cheese

1½ cups buttered bread crumbs

1. Preheat oven to 325 ° F.
2. In a 9x13 baking dish, layer broccoli then chicken.
3. Mix together cream of chicken soup, mayonnaise, lemon juice & curry powder.
4. Pour mixture of top of broccoli & chicken.
5. Top with cheese and bread crumbs and cover with foil
6. Bake in preheated oven for 25 to 30 minutes.
7. Remove foil for the last ten minutes of baking.

Recipe courtesy of Sherry Poulsen

Chefnotes

Can also use fresh broccoli.

Chicken and Broccoli Casserole

W hen Papa Dave's sister April was getting married she had her wedding lunch at Mona's house and Mona and I cooked the meal. April wanted to have this recipe for the lunch and gave us the recipe to make. It was so good and became one of my favorites.

4 cups chicken breasts, roasted chicken, or leftover chicken

Dried onions, optional

Salt, optional

2 (10-ounce) packages chopped broccoli, cooked

2 (10.5-ounce) cans cream of chicken soup

1 cup cheddar cheese, grated

½ cup mayonnaise

1 teaspoon lemon juice

¼ teaspoon curry powder

½ cup bread crumbs

1. Preheat oven to 350 ° F.
2. If using raw chicken, bring water to boil in a large saucepan; add chicken, dried onions, and salt and boil until chicken is tender; drain.
3. Place broccoli on the bottom of a 9x13 casserole dish.
4. Layer cooked chicken on top of broccoli.
5. In a small bowl mix together cream of chicken soup, cheese, mayonnaise, lemon juice, and curry powder.
6. Pour mixture over chicken and sprinkle bread crumbs on top.
7. Bake in preheated oven for 30 minutes.

Recipe courtesy of Sandy Newton

Chefnotes

Can be prepared then frozen before cooking. Add 15 minutes to cooking time when cooking from frozen.

Barbara Robinson's Chicken and Rice

4 tablespoons butter

1 (10.5-ounce) can cream of chicken soup

1 (10.5-ounce) can cream of mushroom soup

1 (10.5-ounce) can cream of celery soup

1 cup rice, uncooked (NOT instant or quick cooking)

1 fryer chicken (See "Food for Thought" note below)

1. Preheat oven to 300 to 325 ° F.

2. Melt butter in a casserole dish. In a large bowl mix remaining ingredients, except chicken, and pour mixture into casserole dish. Break the chicken into pieces, salt and pepper, and place over rice mixture. Cover and bake for 2 hours, uncovering for the last 20 minutes.

Recipe courtesy of Becky Robinson – from Barbara Robinson

Food for Thought

The USDA defines a fryer chicken as a whole young bird between 7 to 10 weeks old and weighing between 2-1/2 and 4-1/2 pounds. I prefer to use boneless chicken breasts.

One Dish Chicken & Rice Casserole

When I am asked to take a meal to someone in need and I don't have a lot of time to prepare, this is my perfect go to. Put it all in a disposable aluminum pan & deliver the meal hot & ready to eat, or uncooked for the recipient to cook at their preferred dinner time. I like to additionally give some rolls and a bagged salad kit and call it a good meal! Also, no dishes to have to track down later.

3 to 5 boneless skinless chicken breasts
1½ cups parboiled or white rice
1 cup water
1 cup milk
2 (10.5-ounce) cans cream of chicken soup
½ teaspoon salt
½ teaspoon black pepper
Seasoning of choice for chicken (ranch, lemon pepper, monterey chicken, etc)

1. Preheat oven to 375 ° F.
2. In a 9x13 baking dish add rice, water, milk, cream of chicken soup, salt, and pepper.
3. Lightly whisk together, mixture does not need to be fully incorporated.
4. Clean and trim chicken breasts, season each heavily on both sides.
5. Optionally, you can slice the chicken breasts in half before seasoning if thinner chicken is preferred.
6. Place chicken on top of the rice mixture in baking dish.
7. Bake for 45 to 60 mins or until rice is soft and chicken is fully cooked.

Recipe courtesy of Jo Jacobs

Food for Thought

We use parboiled rice because we find it gives a heartier texture similar to brown rice, but takes only as long as white rice to cook.

Chefnotes

We like using ranch seasoning best. Lemon pepper is another favorite. Experiment with any seasoning you like.
Feel free to adjust the number of chicken breasts to fit the number of people being served.

Great Grandma Marie's Stuffing Casserole

makes 6 to 8 servings   prep time: 30 minutes   cook time: 35 minutes   total time: 65 minutes

When I came into the family it seemed that every Newton family get together featured this chicken dish. I asked for the recipe, and after making it a few times I started making improvements. It has become the go-to when taking dinner to someone in need. This with green beans and a can of cranberry sauce. Done! Also, be warned, if you make this for dinner for another family and then try to feed your family something else, they'll be grumpy ... so just make two!

Boneless, skinless chicken, cubed

Butter

Salt and black pepper, to taste

Garlic powder, to taste

Dried cranberries

Parsley

Apple juice

Slices of Swiss cheese, optional

2 (10.5-ounce) cans cream of chicken soup, divided

Green beans, fresh or canned

2 (6-ounce) packages stuffing mix

1 cup of water

A little butter

1. Preheat oven to 400 ° F.
2. Cut up the desired amount of chicken. Sauté chicken in a pan with a bit of butter. Add salt, pepper, garlic powder, dried cranberries and parsley. Deglaze the pan with a bit of apple juice.
3. Layer partially cooked chicken and spices in a 9x13 pan.
4. If using, add a layer of cheese on top of the chicken.
5. Next, spread one can of cream soup on top of the chicken and cheese.
6. Place green beans along both short edges of the pan, leaving the middle open.
7. Sprinkle the stuffing mix on top of the soup in the middle of the pan, between the green beans.
8. Mix the remaining can of soup with 1 cup of water and pour over the dry stuffing mix.
9. Cover the pan with foil and place in preheated oven. Cook for approximately 35 minutes, removing the cover for the last 10 minutes of baking to let it brown and crisp on the top. Be sure chicken is fully cooked, so that it reaches an internal temperature of 165 ° F.

Recipe courtesy of Erin Newton – from Marie Newton

Food for Thought

Serve with cranberry sauce.
Can substitute other cheeses for the Swiss cheese.
Instead of cream of chicken soup you can instead use other cream soups such as cream of celery or cream of mushroom, or a combination of cream soups.

Hamburger Noodle Casserole

makes 10 servings

1 pound hamburger, browned

2 medium onions, chopped

2 tablespoons minced pimento

¾ cup uncooked rice

1 (10.5-ounce) can cream of chicken soup

1 (10.5-ounce) can cream of mushroom soup

2 soup cans of water

2 tablespoons soy sauce

1 (5-ounce) can chow mein noodles

1. Preheat oven to 350°F.
2. Mix together all ingredients except chow mein noodles. Bake in a covered pan (approximately 8" x 14") at 350°F for 45 minutes. Cook an additional 10 minutes uncovered.
3. Just before serving, sprinkle with chow mein noodles.

Recipe courtesy of Becky Robinson

Full-O-Boloney Casserole

When my kids were little, one day Ben asked what we were having for dinner and I jokingly told him we were having medicine. So from then on we called this casserole medicine.

3 to 4 potatoes cubed

5 to 6 hot dogs

¼ cup minced green peppers

1 (10.5-ounce) can cream of mushroom soup

1 (8-ounce) package frozen peas

1 cup cheese

1. Place potatoes in a microwave safe dish that can be covered, and cook in microwave for 7 to 8 minutes.
2. Mix in remaining ingredients, except cheese, cover, and cook in microwave for 10 to 15 minutes until potatoes are fully cooked.
3. Sprinkle cheese on top of the casserole and cook an additional 1 minute to melt cheese.

Recipe courtesy of Sandy Newton

Sandy's Enchilada Casserole

makes 4 to 6 servings

1 pound ground beef

1 medium onion

1 clove garlic, crushed

1 teaspoon black pepper

2½ teaspoon chili powder

⅔ cup water

1 8 ounce can tomato sauce

¼ teaspoon salt

6 (8-inch) tortillas, broken into bite-sized pieces

2 cups shredded mild cheddar or

Colby-Monterey Jack cheese

1. In a sauté pan or frying pan cook ground beef, and onion until beef is brown and onions are cooked through.
2. Stir in garlic, pepper, chili powder, water, tomato sauce, and salt and cook 5 to to minutes.
3. In a microwave-safe casserole dish add a layer of tortillas, then meat, then cheese. Continue layering until all ingredients have been used, ensuring that the top layer is cheese.
4. Heat covered in the microwave on medium high for 10 to 12 minutes until the cheese melts.

Recipe courtesy of Sandy Newton

The Best Tater Tot Casserole

1 pound ground beef

½ onion, diced

2 cloves garlic, minced

1 tablespoon Worcestershire sauce

1 (14.5-ounce) can green beans, drained

1 (10.5-ounce) can cream of chicken soup

1 cup sour cream

2 cups shredded cheddar cheese

2 cups frozen tater tots

Salt and black pepper, to taste

1. Preheat oven to 375 ° F.
2. Lightly grease a 9x9 baking dish with cooking spray.
3. Brown the ground beef in a medium skillet over medium high heat. Drain excess fat.
4. Add the onions to the skillet and saute for 4 to 5 minutes until translucent.
5. Add the garlic and cook for another minute.
6. Stir in the Worcestershire sauce and season with salt and pepper.
7. Combine the cream of chicken soup and sour cream in a small bowl, and set aside.
8. Transfer the ground beef mixture to the prepared baking dish and spread evenly.
9. Top with the soup and sour cream mixture, followed by the green beans seasoned with salt and pepper, and then the cheese.
10. Finally, top with a single layer of tater tots.
11. Bake for 35 to 40 minutes or until tater tots are golden brown and cheese is melted.

Recipe courtesy of Jen Burge

Chapter 10

Slow Cooker Meals

ONCE UPON A TIME there was a little girl who was starving. She wanted to eat alota, alota food.

The next day she woke up and she was so hungry that she had a dream and she woke up and there was a buncha buncha food. So she ate all of that and then she went downstairs in the kitchen to get some food and then she checked every cupboard and she said that there was no food. So she went outside and killed some stuff so she could have some food.

And then the next day, she saw a bunch of turkeys that she killed and she was so happy about herself that she got some turkeys. So she ate that and the next day she ate all of that and then she was never starving again!

The End

Annabelle Schultz - Age 5

Mississippi Roast

makes 6 servings

We had friends that introduced us to this delicious recipe. They made it every Sunday, which is usually when we ate dinner together.

1 (4-pound) beef chuck roast

¼ cup butter

5 pepperoncini peppers

1 (1-ounce) packet ranch dressing mix

1 (1-ounce) packet dry au jus mix

1. Place roast in a slow cooker. Form a pocket in the top of roast and place butter, pepperoncini peppers, ranch dressing mix, and au jus mix in the pocket.

2. Cook on Low for 8 hours.

Recipe courtesy of Amy Trent – adapted from www.allrecipes.com/recipe/246721

Chefnotes

Substitute beef round or beef brisket for the beef chuck, if desired.

Chicken Curry

1 (14.5-ounce) can chicken broth

1 (10.5-ounce) can cream of chicken

1 (10.5-ounce) can cream of mushroom

1 (20-ounce) can pineapple tidbits with juice

2 cups chicken breasts, diced

½ teaspoon ground ginger

¼ teaspoon curry powder

¼ cup green onions, sliced

Slivered almonds, to taste

1. Combine all ingredients in a slow cooker and mix together. Cook on low for 6 to 8 hours or on high for 4 to 6 hours.

2. Serve over rice.

Recipe courtesy of Sherry Poulsen

Michelle Robinson's Italian Chicken Stroganoff
makes 4 to 5 servings

This is one of my daughter's favorite recipes. Who doesn't like a delicious, but quick and easy to fix recipe?

2 (10.5-ounce) cans cream of chicken soup

½ to 1 soup can of milk

1 (0.7-ounce) package dry Italian dressing seasoning mix

1 (8-ounce) package cream cheese, softened

4 to 5 chicken breasts

1. Mix all ingredients except chicken in slow cooker, then add chicken and cook 4 to 6 hours.

2. Remove chicken and shred with a fork.

3. Return chicken to slow cooker, mix together, and serve over rice, egg noodles, or mashed potatoes.

Recipe courtesy of Becky Robinson

Creamy Chicken and Rice

This is a tasty recipe and I often use it for Hawaiian Haystacks. You can shred the chicken once it is cooked or you can leave it as is.

Slow Cooker:

6 chicken breasts

1 (0.7-ounce) package dry Italian dressing

2 tablespoons butter

Salt and black pepper, to taste.

Sauce:

1 (10.5-ounce) can cream of chicken soup

1 cup chicken broth

1 (8-ounce) package cream cheese

1 teaspoon dried onion

Rice

1. Add chicken, Italian dressing and butter to a slow cooker and cook on low for 6 to 8 hours or on high for 4 to 6 hours.

2. Mix together cream of chicken soup, broth, cheese and dried onion in a saucepan.

3. Pour sauce over chicken and serve with rice.

Recipe courtesy of Jen Burge

Salsa Chicken Tacos

*T*his salsa taco recipe is more than just throwing a jar of salsa in to cook with your chicken. With a few added spices it really elevates this dish and makes it really tasty, all while still being a simple and easy recipe.

1½ pounds boneless skinless chicken breasts

2 teaspoons chili powder

1 teaspoon ground cumin

½ teaspoon ground coriander

¼ teaspoon salt, to taste

¼ teaspoon black pepper, to taste

1 clove garlic, minced

1 cup salsa

2 tablespoons chopped cilantro

1. Place chicken in Instant Pot or slow cooker.
2. In a small bowl mix together chili powder, cumin, coriander, salt, and pepper.
3. Sprinkle mixture evenly over both sides of chicken and sprinkle garlic over chicken. Then pour salsa over chicken to cover.
4. Close lid, turn vent to "sealing" and set Instant Pot to "manual" setting for 13 minutes. If using a slow cooker cook for 5 to 6 hours on low heat.
5. Once the cycle is complete use quick release method for Instant Pot.
6. Remove chicken and let cool several minutes on cutting board then shred into pieces and return to juices in the pot.
7. Sprinkle in cilantro, toss chicken to coat. Season with more salt if desired.
8. Lift shredded chicken with tongs and allow excess liquid to run off, then place in tortilla with desired toppings.

Recipe courtesy of Jen Burge

Chefnotes

I use Herdez brand Roasted Salsa Roja jarred salsa.

Jen's Tikka Masala

*F*or much of my life I was never a huge fan of Indian food because I never knew what to order or what was best. However, I changed my mind when I met my friend Heather and she introduced me to this recipe and her love of Indian food. This Indian recipe is as easy as they come and very flavorful.

1 (29-ounce) can tomato sauce
1 (14-ounce) can crushed tomatoes
1½ to 2 pounds chicken breast, chunked
1 small onion, chopped
4 cloves garlic, minced
2 tablespoons butter
1 tablespoon cumin
1 tablespoon white sugar
2 teaspoons paprika
1 teaspoon ground ginger
½ teaspoon curry powder
½ teaspoon cayenne pepper
½ teaspoon cinnamon
½ teaspoon salt

¼ teaspoon black pepper
¼ teaspoon turmeric
1 cup heavy cream
Cilantro

1. Combine tomato sauce, crushed tomatoes, chicken, onion, garlic and butter in a slow cooker.
2. In a separate small bowl mix together all the spices (remaining ingredients except cream and cilantro), then add to the slow cooker and mix in.
3. Cook on low for 6 to 8 hours or on high for 4 to 6 hours.
4. Just before serving stir in 1 cup heavy cream.
5. Serve with rice and or naan bread and garnish with cilantro.

Recipe courtesy of Jen Burge

Erin's Sweet Potato Coconut Curry

cook time: 5ish hours

1 to 2 onions, chopped

4 sweet potatoes (add more if not including chicken)

4 to 5 boneless, skinless chicken breasts (optional)

3 to 4 cloves of garlic, minced

1 teaspoon salt

1 teaspoon black pepper

5 teaspoons curry powder

1 teaspoon chili powder

1 teaspoon ground coriander

1 teaspoon ground turmeric

1 teaspoon ground cumin

1 teaspoon fenugreek

1 (2-inch) thumb of ginger, minced, or 1 teaspoon dried ginger

1 teaspoon asafetida

1 teaspoon cinnamon

1 teaspoon caraway

½ teaspoon cloves

Pinch of nutmeg

2 (14.5-ounce) cans diced tomato

1 to 2 (13.5-ounce) cans of coconut milk

1. Dice onion and place in slow cooker.

2. Peel sweet potatoes, and dice them into various-sized pieces. Place them in the slow cooker on top of the onions.

3. Cube the chicken and place atop the sweet potatoes in the slow cooker.

4. Now, sprinkle, dump, splash or otherwise add all the other ingredients to the vessel. Add all spices, to taste.

5. Put the lid on the slow cooker, turn to high and carry on.

6. Allow to cook for about 5 hours on high.

7. If adding spinach or kale stir in about 30 minutes before cooking is complete.

8. Before serving, stir the curry and the sweet potatoes will disintegrate a bit and making it lovely and creamy.

9. Serve over rice optionally topped with golden raisins, cilantro, coconut flakes, and green salsa.

Recipe courtesy of Erin Newton

Food for Thought

I am not a scientific cook, and these measurements are just a guide, and should be adjusted to suit your tastes. I add spices until it smells and tastes like I want it to. Cook by the spirit sometime, it may surprise you.

Chefnotes

👒 Can also add baby kale or spinach.
Dice the sweet potatoes in various sizes to add texture to the curry.

Cafe Rio Shredded Pork

2 (12-ounce) cans of coke
½ teaspoon garlic salt
½ cup brown sugar
¼ cup water
2 pounds pork
½ cup coke
1 (4-ounce) can diced green chiles

¾ can red enchilada sauce
1 cup brown sugar

1. Combine coke, garlic salt, 1/2 cup brown sugar, water, and pork in a slow cooker. Cook on low for 6 to 7 hours.
2. Drain meat and combine with 1/2 cup coke, chiles, enchilada sauce and 1 cup brown sugar. Heat until warm.

Recipe courtesy of Stacy Schultz

Slow Cooker Easy Baked Potato Soup

10 red potatoes, cut into cubes
3 tablespoons all-purpose flour
¾ cup real bacon bits
1 small red onion, chopped
1 clove garlic, minced
2 tablespoons chicken bouillon granules
1 tablespoon ranch dressing mix
2 teaspoons dried parsley
1 teaspoon seasoned salt
½ teaspoon ground black pepper
3 cups water
1 cup half-and-half

½ cup shredded Cheddar cheese, or to taste
¼ cup chopped green onion, or to taste

1. Put potatoes in the bottom of your slow cooker crock. Scatter flour over the potatoes; toss to coat.
2. Scatter bacon bits, red onion, garlic, chicken bouillon, ranch dressing mix, parsley, seasoned salt, and black pepper over the potatoes.
3. Pour water into the slow cooker.
4. Cook on Low 7 to 9 hours.
5. Pour half-and-half into the soup; cook another 15 minutes.
6. Garnish with Cheddar cheese and green onion to serve.

Recipe courtesy of Amy Trent – adapted from www.allrecipes.com/recipe/220910

Chefnotes

Alternately, you can cook this on high for 4 to 5 hours.

Main Dishes

*I*F YOUR ENTREE ever flops, don't worry or stress. Simply enact the McDonald's clause. Shortly after getting married (probably after the second time I accidentally dumped the noodles into the disposal instead of draining them) Mark and I came up with the McDonald's clause.

You should know three things for this to make sense. First, neither of us particularly cares for McDonald's. Second, neither of us particularly wanted to go out after finally getting home from a long day of school. Lastly, finances were rather tight since Mark was still in school.

The clause was this: If the dinner we made ever really and truly flopped so as to be inedible, we could go to McDonald's.

We have only had to invoke the McDonald's clause once. My advice: just don't buy whole wheat pasta noodles.

Amy Trent

Jen's Sweet and Sour Meatballs

*T*his recipe has been a favorite of mine ever since I was a teenager and found it in one of my mom's cookbooks. It's a comfort food for me and is at the very top of my list of favorite dinners.

<u>Meatballs:</u>
1 pound ground beef
½ cup bread crumbs
¼ cup milk
2 tablespoons chopped onions
1 teaspoon salt
½ teaspoon Worcestershire sauce
1 large egg
<u>Sauce:</u>
¾ cup brown sugar
2 tablespoons cornstarch
1 (20-ounce) can pineapple tidbits with juice

1 small (6 to 8-ounce) can of pineapple juice
⅓ cup vinegar
2 tablespoons soy sauce
1 green pepper, chopped

1. Mix together ground beef, bread crumbs, milk, onions, salt, Worcestershire sauce, and egg and shape into balls about 1 inch in size.
2. Brown meatballs in a skillet, drain the fat, and set aside.
3. In a small saucepan mix together remaining ingredients, and bring to a boil.
4. Add meatballs and simmer for 10 minutes.
5. Serve over rice.

Recipe courtesy of Jen Burge

Chefnotes

I sometimes improvise by using water and extra vinegar if I don't have a can of pineapple juice.

Stacy's Sweet and Sour Meatballs

makes 5 to 6 servings

Meatballs:
1 pound ground beef
1 tablespoon dehydrated onion
½ teaspoon black pepper
1 teaspoon salt
1 large egg, beaten
¼ cup breadcrumbs

Sauce:
¾ cup brown sugar
3 tablespoons all-purpose flour
1½ cup pineapple juice
¼ cup vinegar
3 tablespoons soy sauce

Optional:
Carrots, cut up
Onions

Bell Peppers
Pineapple

1. In a large bowl, combine beef, onion, pepper, salt, egg, and breadcrumbs.

2. Shape the meat into 1-inch balls and place on cookie sheet lined with foil and the sprayed with non-stick spray.

3. Broil in oven for 5 to 7 minutes, until golden brown

4. Meanwhile, in a large skillet, whisk together brown sugar, flour, pineapple juice, vinegar, and soy sauce.

5. Add the meatballs to the sauce and let simmer for 20 minutes, stirring occasionally.

6. Optionally, also add carrots, onions, bell peppers, and pineapple to the sauce before simmering.

Recipe courtesy of Stacy Schultz – from Becky Evans

Food for Thought

One can of pineapple will yield 1 cup of pineapple juice.
Can be frozen with sauce and meatballs mixed.

Meatloaf

This recipe came from a cooking class that Ben, Stacy, Jenny and Josh went to when they were kids. During the class they made this in a muffin tin, with rice and vegetables in some of the muffin slots. We never made it that way. It still is a family favorite.

½ pound lean ground beef

¼ cup bread crumbs

1 tablespoon chopped onion

1 large egg, beaten

¼ teaspoons salt

Dash of black pepper

¼ cup brown sugar

1 tablespoon Worcestershire sauce

1 tablespoon prepared mustard

¼ cup ketchup

½ teaspoon nutmeg

1. Grease a loaf pan and preheat oven to 350 ° F.
2. In a medium bowl, combine ground beef, bread crumbs, onion, egg, salt, and pepper.
3. Press meat mixture into loaf pan.
4. In a small bowl combine brown sugar, Worcestershire sauce, mustard, ketchup, and nutmeg. Blend well.
5. Pour the sauce over the meat.
6. Bake for 30 minutes.

Recipe courtesy of Sandy Newton – adapted from Dinner in a Muffin Tin

Cajun Shrimp and Sausage Skillet

So delicious!!! This is one of the easiest recipes I have and it's nice because you really can throw in any vegetables you want. A great way to use your garden vegetables and a great last minute meal.

1 pound large shrimp

14 ounces pork or chicken sausage, sliced

2 medium-sized zucchinis, sliced

2 medium sized yellow squashes, sliced

½ bunch asparagus, sliced into thirds

2 red bell peppers, chopped into chunks

Salt and black pepper, to taste

2 tablespoons olive oil

2 tablespoons Cajun Seasoning

1. Put all the meats and vegetables in a large skillet. Drizzle olive oil over the top and toss to coat. Add the salt, pepper and Cajun seasoning (extra if you want) and toss to coat.

2. Cook on medium heat for about 5 to 7 minutes until the shrimp is pink and the vegetables are tender.

Recipe courtesy of Jen Burge

Chefnotes

I use frozen, peeled, deveined, tail off shrimp, and Weber N'Orleans Cajun Seasoning for this recipe.

Cajun Spice Mix

makes ¼ cup

See the recipe for the Cajun Chicken Pasta

2 teaspoons salt

2 teaspoons garlic powder

2½ teaspoons paprika

1 teaspoon ground black pepper

1 teaspoon onion powder

1 teaspoon cayenne pepper

1¼ teaspoons dried oregano

1¼ teaspoons dried thyme

½ teaspoon red pepper flakes (Optional)

1. Stir together salt, garlic powder, paprika, black pepper, onion powder, cayenne pepper, oregano, thyme, and red pepper flakes until evenly blended. Store in an airtight container.

Recipe courtesy of Amy Trent – from www.allrecipes.com/recipe/149221

Cajun Chicken Pasta

makes 2 servings

This is an easy wonderful recipe. It's delicious! Great for taking to people as well.

4 ounces linguine pasta

2 boneless, skinless chicken breast halves, sliced into thin strips

2 teaspoons Cajun seasoning

2 tablespoons butter

1 green bell pepper, chopped

½ red bell pepper, chopped

4 fresh mushrooms, sliced

1 green onion, minced

1½ cups heavy cream

¼ teaspoon dried basil

¼ teaspoon lemon pepper

¼ teaspoon salt

⅛ teaspoon garlic powder

⅛ teaspoon ground black pepper

2 tablespoons grated Parmesan cheese

1. Bring a large pot of lightly salted water to a boil. Add linguini pasta, and cook for 8 to 10 minutes, or until al dente; drain.

2. Meanwhile, place chicken and Cajun seasoning in a bowl, and toss to coat.

3. In a large skillet over medium heat, saute chicken in butter until no longer pink and juices run clear, about 5 to 7 minutes. Add green and red bell peppers, sliced mushrooms and green onions; cook for 2 to 3 minutes. Reduce heat, and stir in heavy cream. Season the sauce with basil, lemon pepper, salt, garlic powder and ground black pepper, and heat through.

4. In a large bowl, toss linguini with sauce. Sprinkle with grated Parmesan cheese.

Recipe courtesy of Amy Trent – adapted from www.allrecipes.com/recipe/12009

Monterey Grilled Chicken

Chicken Marinade:
¼ cup olive oil
2 tablespoons soy sauce
2 teaspoons McCormick Montreal Steak
  Seasoning

Chicken:
4 chicken breasts, marinated
¼ cup barbecue sauce
1 cup colby and jack cheese, shredded
1 (10-ounce) can Ro-Tel tomatoes with green
  chilies
Sliced green onions

¼ cup real bacon bits

1. Mix olive oil, soy sauce, and steak seasoning.
2. Marinate the chicken in the mixture for 30 to 60 minutes.
3. Preheat oven to 400 ° F.
4. Grill the chicken on an outdoor grill until no longer pink, and place on baking sheet or pan covered with foil.
5. Top each chicken breast with barbecue sauce, cheese, tomatoes, green onions and bacon bits.
6. Place in preheated oven and bake until cheese is melted (about 5 to 10 minutes).

Recipe courtesy of Jen Burge

Chili Lime Chicken

2 to 2½ pounds chicken thighs or boneless
  skinless chicken breasts
½ cup lime juice
3 teaspoons lime zest
¼ cup olive oil
4 tablespoons fresh cilantro
2 jalapenos, chopped finely
4 garlic cloves, chopped finely
1 tablespoon honey
2 teaspoons salt
1 teaspoon chili powder

1. Rinse the chicken, pat dry with paper towel and set aside.
2. Combine all the rest of the ingredients in a large bowl and mix until well combined.
3. Add the chicken to the marinade, make sure to stir and coat evenly.
4. Marinate chicken for 2 hours.
5. Fire up the grill, brush a little bit of oil on the surface. Add a little bit of the garlic, cilantro and jalapeno from the marinade on top of the chicken and grill until golden brown and charred on both sides.
6. Serve and enjoy.

Recipe courtesy of Jen Burge

Chicken Enchilada Skillet

makes 6 servings

*A*gain, easy has me sold. Rolling up enchiladas is harder than just cooking the enchilada innards and dipping chips to eat.

Cooking spray

12 corn tortillas, torn into bite-size pieces

3 cups shredded cooked chicken

1 (10-ounce) can diced tomatoes & green chilies, undrained

1 (10-ounce) can red enchilada sauce

1 (8-ounce) can tomato sauce

1 cup shredded cheddar and Monterey jack blend cheese, divided

1. Spray large nonstick skillet with cooking spray. Add tortilla pieces and chicken; mix well. Cook over medium-high heat 5 minutes or until hot, stirring frequently.

2. Pour undrained tomatoes and enchilada and tomato sauces over chicken mixture in skillet. Mix well. Sprinkle 1/2 cup cheese over chicken mixture. Cover skillet; cook 5 minutes or until hot, stirring occasionally. Sprinkle with remaining 1/2 cup cheese. Serve immediately.

Recipe courtesy of Amy Trent – adapted from www.allrecipes.com/recipe/245515

Chefnotes

Leave out the corn tortillas and just dip chips. I might simmer a little longer to make it easier to dip.

Easy Pineapple Chicken

*Y*ou had me at easy. This recipe lives up to its name, and it doesn't taste too bad either.

3 tablespoons soy sauce

3 tablespoons olive oil, divided

½ teaspoon paprika

Salt, to taste

1 pound boneless, skinless chicken breasts, cut into strips

1 red bell pepper, cubed

1 bunch scallions, trimmed and sliced into ½-inch lengths

1 (12-ounce) can pineapple chunks, drained with juice reserved

1 tablespoon cornstarch

1. Combine soy sauce, 2 tablespoons olive oil, paprika, and salt in a bowl. Add chicken strips and let marinate while preparing the remaining ingredients.

2. Heat the remaining 1 tablespoon of olive oil in a wok or large skillet. Add bell pepper and stir-fry for 3 minutes. Add scallions and cook for 2 more minutes. Remove chicken from marinade and add to the wok; discard marinade. Cook, stirring occasionally, until chicken is cooked through and no longer pink in the centre, 10 to 15 minutes.

3. Combine pineapple juice and cornstarch in a bowl; mix together. Add pineapple chunks to the skillet and cook for 2 to 3 minutes. Pour in pineapple juice mixture and bring to a boil. Simmer until sauce has thickened, about 3 minutes.

Recipe courtesy of Amy Trent – adapted from www.allrecipes.com/recipe/262797

Chicken Crescents

makes 16 crescents

*L*ove it because they taste wonderful!

Crescents:
6 ounces cream cheese
2 tablespoons butter, melted
2 cups cooked chicken, cubed
¼ teaspoon salt
⅛ teaspoon black pepper
2 tablespoons milk
1 tablespoon onion, chopped
½ cup mushrooms, sliced
2 (8-ounce) cans refrigerated crescent rolls
Italian dressing poured on a plate

Gourmet sauce:
mushrooms, sliced and sautéed (optional)
1 (10.5-ounce) can cream of mushroom soup
1 (10.5-ounce) can cream of chicken soup
½ cup sour cream
½ cup grated cheddar cheese
½ cup mayonnaise

dash of garlic powder

1. Preheat oven to 350 ° F.
2. In a medium bowl, mix together melted butter and softened cream cheese. Add chicken, salt, pepper, milk, onion and mushrooms, and mix to combine.
3. Separate first can of dough into 8 triangles and spread about 1/4 cup chicken mixture onto each. Fold each, sealing the dough. Repeat for second can of dough and remaining chicken mixture.
4. Brush folded dough with melted butter and roll in Italian dressing. Place on an ungreased baking sheet.
5. Bake at 350 ° F for about 40 minutes or until golden brown.
6. For the sauce, mix remaining ingredients in a medium saucepan, and heat on low.
7. Pour a little of the gourmet sauce on the crescents before serving.

Recipe courtesy of Rick Poulsen

Chicken Parmigiana

makes 4 servings   prep time: 1 hour   cook time: 1 hour and 15 minutes

*T*his is a Guy Fieri recipe. Love him or hate him but brining the chicken is genius and I could eat this everyday.

4 (5-ounce) boneless, skinless, trimmed chicken breasts

½ cup kosher salt

½ cup white sugar

1½ cups all-purpose flour

2 large eggs

¼ cup milk

1½ cups dried bread crumbs

1½ cups panko bread crumbs

¼ teaspoon dried oregano

¼ teaspoon dried basil

1 teaspoon dried parsley

1 teaspoon fine sea salt

½ teaspoon freshly ground black pepper

1 pound fresh mozzarella cheese, sliced

¼ pound Parmigiano-Reggiano, grated

Olive oil, for frying (about 2 cups)

1 pound penne rigate, cooked al dente

Tomato Sauce (recipe follows)

¼ cup minced Italian parsley, for garnish

Tomato Sauce:

2 tablespoons extra-virgin olive oil

1 yellow onion, minced

4 garlic cloves, crushed

6 cups peeled and diced Roma tomatoes

1 tablespoon thinly sliced fresh basil leaves

½ tablespoon chopped fresh oregano leaves

Salt and freshly ground black pepper, to taste

1. Lightly pound the chicken breasts to 1/2-inch thickness. Combine the kosher salt, sugar, and 1 quart of water in a 1-gallon size resealable plastic bag; shake until dissolved. Add the chicken breasts and soak at room temperature for 30 minutes.

2. Place the flour in a medium bowl. Remove the chicken from the brine. Shake off excess moisture and, with tongs, lightly dredge the chicken in the flour. Shake off the excess flour and transfer to a large plate.

3. Mix the eggs and milk in medium bowl and whisk thoroughly. In a separate bowl combine the bread crumbs, oregano, basil, parsley, salt, and pepper. Dredge the chicken in the egg mixture with tongs and let excess mixture drain off. Now dredge the chicken into the bread crumb mixture, and lightly pat down in the bread crumbs to adhere.

4. Preheat the broiler. Let the breaded chicken sit for 5 minutes before frying. In a medium saucepan on medium-high heat, add enough olive oil to come 1/3 up the side of the chicken. Cook the chicken in batches until golden brown on both sides. Remove from the pan when cooked and place on a sheet tray. Repeat with remaining chicken.

5. When all the chicken is cooked, sprinkle mozzarella and Parmesan evenly over the top. Place under the broiler until the cheese melts and is golden brown.

6. Serve chicken over pasta and ladle tomato sauce on top. Garnish with extra Parmesan and parsley.

7. **Tomato Sauce:** Heat the olive oil over medium heat in a saucepan. Add the onions and cook until translucent. Add the garlic and cook until almost brown, then add tomatoes. Saute for 30 minutes over low to medium heat. Add the basil and oregano and continue to cook for 30 minutes longer. Puree in a food mill or let cool and puree in a food processor. Season with salt and pepper.

Recipe courtesy of Rose Frank – from Guy Fieri

Uncle Ben's Dry Rub

*T*his mixture of spices is great to rub on meat before grilling or baking. It was inspired by a rub some friends introduced us to in North Carolina. Mix up a batch, use some, and store the remainder it in airtight container.

1 tablespoon cumin
1 tablespoon paprika
1 tablespoon garlic powder
1 tablespoon onion powder
1 tablespoon chili powder
1 tablespoon brown sugar
2 tablespoons salt
1 teaspoon cayenne pepper

1 teaspoon black pepper
1 teaspoon white pepper

1. Measure all the ingredients into a small bowl and mix to completely combine.

2. Generously rub the mixture all over your chosen meat, getting it into every nook and cranny.

3. Cook meat right away, or refrigerate and cook later.

Recipe courtesy of Ben Newton

Uncle Ben's Grilled Chicken

*U*se the rub above for easy, and tasty grilled chicken. I'll never forget making this chicken in Lake Powell at the grill on the back of the houseboat. Good food. Good times!

Boneless skinless chicken breasts, fresh or thawed, about½ breast per person.
Uncle Ben's Dry Rub

1. The secret to this recipe is filleting the chicken breasts very thin. This is a trick taught to me by by friend Eric Molloy from Ireland. Place a chicken breast flat on a work surface. Place the palm of your left (or non-prominent) hand directly over the breast and press down lightly. With a sharp serrated knife in your other hand carefully slice off the top 1/3 of the chicken breast working right to left (or opposite if left handed). You will be able to feel with your hand pressing down on the chicken how close the knife is to the surface. Continue, cutting the remaining chicken in half, for three thin fillets. Vary the number of cuts to fit the thickness of the chicken breasts.

2. Light barbecue grill.

3. Place a generous amount of the rub in a large bowl. One by one place the chicken fillets into the bowl and rub with the spices to coat well, then place on a plate.

4. Grill fillets over medium heat until chicken is fully cooked.

Recipe courtesy of Ben Newton

Pie Crust

2 cups all-purpose flour

1 teaspoon salt

½ pound (2 sticks) unsalted butter, cold and sliced

⅓ cup ice water

1. Put flour and salt into a food processor fitted with a chopping blade. Process for 10 seconds. Add butter and pulse until the mixture resembles coarse crumbs. Pour in water, 1 tablespoon at a time, and pulse until a dough just forms. May not need all the water. Divide dough into 2 flat discs; wrap in plastic and refrigerate until ready to use.

2. **Roll and blind-bake:** On a lightly floured surface, roll out one of the pastry discs into an 11-inch circle that is about ⅛-inch thick. Reverse the dough onto the rolling pin and unroll it evenly over a 9-inch tart pan. Press the dough lightly into the pan, lifting the edges and working it gently down into the corners of the pan. Trim off excess dough by rolling the pin over the top of the pan.

3. With your thumbs, push the dough ⅛ inch above the edge of the mold, to make an even, rounded rim of dough around the inside circumference of the mold. You can then press a decorative edge around the rim of the pastry with the dull edge of a knife. Chill in refrigerator for about 30 minutes.

4. Preheat oven to 350 ° F. Using a fork, prick the dough evenly all over, but make sure not to go entirely through the dough. Line the shell with parchment and weigh it down with dried beans or rice. Once preheated, place into oven. Bake in preheated oven for about 20 minutes, or until the dough under the parchment is no longer wet. Remove the beans/rice and parchment and continue baking for an additional 5 minutes, until the shell is golden brown.

Recipe courtesy of Ben Newton – from www.cuisinart.com/recipes/desserts/pate-brisee2/

Chicken Pot Pie

makes 8 servings   *prep time: 20 minutes*   *cook time: 50 minutes*   *total time: 1 hour and 10 minutes*

*P*i (π) is a mathematical constant representing the ratio of any circle's circumference to its diameter. It has become customary, especially for the more nerdy-types and their children, to celebrate Pi Day each March 14th (because pi is approximately 3.14). During the Covid-19 pandemic our family had a wonderful Pi Day celebration, where we enjoyed a whole meal of pies, which not only share a name with this constant, and whose circular shape complements its meaning. We had multiple pies for dessert, and this wonderful chicken pot pie for the main course. We hope you enjoy even if it's not Pi Day.

1 pound skinless, boneless chicken breast, cubed

1 cup carrots, sliced

1 cup frozen green peas

½ cup celery, sliced

Water

⅓ cup butter

⅓ cup onion, chopped

⅓ cup all-purpose flour

½ teaspoon salt

¼ teaspoon black pepper

¼ teaspoon celery seed, optional

1 ¾ cups chicken broth

⅔ cup milk

2 9-inch unbaked pie crusts

1. Preheat oven to 425 ° F.

2. In a saucepan, combine chicken, carrots, peas, and celery. Add water to cover and boil for 15 minutes. Remove from heat, drain and set aside.

3. In another saucepan, over medium heat, cook onions in butter until soft and translucent. Stir in flour, salt, pepper, and celery seed, if using. Slowly stir in chicken broth and milk. Simmer over medium-low heat until thick. Remove from heat and set aside.

4. Place the chicken and vegetables in bottom pie crust. Pour the hot liquid mixture over. Cover with top crust, seal edges, and cut away excess dough. Make several small slits in the top to allow steam to escape. Optionally, brush top with egg wash or milk.

5. Bake in the preheated oven for 30 to 35 minutes, or until pastry is golden brown and filling is bubbly. Cool for 10 minutes before serving.

Recipe courtesy of Ben Newton – from www.allrecipes.com/recipe/26317

Sherry's Meat Pie

makes about 2 pies

Sherry is an amazing cook and a lot of my favorites are from her. This recipe has such a unique crust, using potato flakes in it When hamburger goes on sale Stacy and I will get together and make a bunch of them and freeze them to use later. They freeze will and we have a good time together while we make them.

Crust:

¼ cup potato flakes

2 cups all-purpose flour

1 tablespoon white sugar

1 teaspoon cream of tartar

1 teaspoon baking soda

⅓ cup butter or margarine

½ cup milk

¼ cup mayonnaise

Filling:

1 pound ground beef

½ cup chopped onion

1 teaspoon salt

¼ teaspoon black pepper

¾ cup potato flakes

1 large egg

¼ cup ketchup

¼ cup sweet relish

1 tablespoon mustard

1 cup cheddar cheese, grated

¼ cup potato flakes

2 tablespoons melted butter

Milk

1. Preheat oven to 375 ° F.
2. To make the pie crusts, in a medium bowl mix together potato flakes, flour, sugar, cream of tartar, and baking soda.
3. Cut the butter or margarine into the flour mixture until it resembles coarse crumbs.
4. Add milk and mayonnaise, mix to form a soft dough, and set aside.
5. To make the meat filling, in a fry pan or saute pan cook ground beef, onion, salt, and pepper until well browned.
6. Remove from heat and stir in potato flakes, egg, ketchup, sweet relish, and mustard.
7. Divide dough in half, and roll out each to form a pie crust.
8. Press one pie crust into a pie pan, and fill with meat filling.
9. Sprinkle with grated cheese.
10. Add top crust over cheese and pinch top and bottom crusts together around the edge.
11. Mix together 1/4 cup potato flakes and melted butter.
12. Brush crust with milk and sprinkle with potato flake topping.
13. Bake for 25 to 30 minutes.

Recipe courtesy of Sandy Newton – from Sherry Poulsen

Chefnotes

The meat pies freeze well, and can be made in bulk. 5 batches will make 8 9-inch pies.

CHAPTER 11. MAIN DISHES

Newton Family Creamed Tuna on Toast

When I was growing up, I think we ate this for dinner about once a week. Never got tired of it! Applesauce on top? You bet! It's just not the same without it.

¼ cup (½ stick) butter

¼ cup all-purpose flour

3 cups milk

1 (5-ounce) can tuna fish

1 cup frozen peas

Buttered toast

Applesauce

1. In a large saucepan melt butter over medium heat. Add flour and stir to make a smooth paste.

2. Cook for 2 to 3 minutes while stirring.

3. Add milk and mix to combine.

4. Mix in tuna and peas, and stir until mixture comes to a boil.

5. If too thin, add a mixture of cornstarch and water and bring back to a boil. If too thick, add milk. Careful: mixture will thicken some as it cools.

6. Serve over buttered toast and top with applesauce.

Recipe courtesy of Dave Newton

Food for Thought

Don't knock the applesauce till you try it!

Chefnotes

I don't drain the tuna fish, figuring the juice adds flavor. I also prefer frozen peas ... to icky canned ones!

Curried Chicken

makes 6 servings

*E*asy + Yum = something I'll cook again.

1 whole chicken, cut into 8 pieces with skin removed

Salt and ground black pepper, to taste

1 tablespoon paprika, or to taste

1 tablespoon butter

1 apple, cored and chopped

1 onion, chopped

1 tablespoon curry powder, or more to taste

1 (10.75-ounce) can cream of mushroom soup

1 cup half-and-half cream

1. Preheat an oven to 350 ° F.
2. Arrange the chicken pieces in a single layer in a 9x13-inch baking dish. Season the chicken liberally with salt, pepper, and the paprika; set aside.
3. Melt the butter in a skillet over medium heat. Add the apple and onion to the melted butter, season with the curry powder, and cook and stir until the apple and onion are tender, 7 to 10 minutes. Stir the mushroom soup and half-and-half into the mixture until completely combined; spoon over the chicken pieces.
4. Bake in the preheated oven until no longer pink at the bone and the juices run clear, about 75 minutes. An instant-read thermometer inserted into the thickest part of the thigh, near the bone should read 180 ° F.

Recipe courtesy of Amy Trent – from www.allrecipes.com/recipe/216795

Coconut Chicken Curry

makes 4 servings   prep time: 15 minutes   cook time: 15 minutes   total time: 30 minutes

*T*his is one of my favorite dinners that my mom makes.

3 tablespoons coconut oil, separated

½ medium yellow onion diced (about ½ cup)

3 cloves garlic, minced (about 1½ teaspoons)

2 tablespoons fresh ginger, finely minced (from a 1½ inch piece)

2 teaspoons yellow curry powder

3 tablespoons red curry paste, adjust to desired spice level

2 teaspoons ground coriander

1 large red bell pepper

1 pound boneless skinless chicken breast or thighs, cut into 1 inch pieces

1 teaspoon fine sea salt, to taste

½ teaspoon freshly ground pepper, to taste

1 (13.5-ounce) can full-fat coconut milk

1 tablespoon lime juice

1 to 2 tablespoons brown sugar, to taste

2 teaspoons fish sauce, optional

¼ cup cilantro and/or basil, diced

Peanuts or cashews, chopped, optional

1. Start by prepping ingredients: Dice the onion, mince the garlic, and mince the ginger. I peel the ginger with a spoon or vegetable peeler and then finely mince it. Thinly slice the red bell pepper into long vertical strips and then cut those strips in half horizontally.

2. Heat 2 tablespoons coconut oil in a large deep skillet over medium-high heat. Add the onion and saute for 3 to 5 minutes or until onions begin to turn golden. Add the garlic and ginger; stir to coat everything with the oil. Lower the heat to low and add in the curry powder, red curry paste, and coriander. Stir often for 2 to 3 minutes or until lightly toasted and fragrant.

3. Return the heat to medium high. Add in the remaining 1 tablespoon coconut oil and the red bell pepper. Stir for 1 to 2 minutes and then add in the bite-sized pieces of chicken. Sprinkle on salt and pepper to taste. Cook, stirring often for about 4 to 5 minutes or until the chicken is browned on both sides, but not cooked through.

4. Pour in the coconut milk, lime juice, and brown sugar. Stir until chicken is cooked through (juices run clear and it is cooked to 165 ° F) and curry is slightly thickened. If desired, stir in the fish sauce.

5. Serve over cooked basmati rice. Garnish with cilantro, basil, and optionally peanuts or cashews. Serve with naan bread and additional lime wedges, if desired.

Recipe courtesy of McKay Burge – from www.chelseasmessyapron.com/coconut-chicken-curry

Food for Thought

Don't use lite coconut milk.

Chefnotes

For a thicker sauce, you can remove 1 to 2 tablespoons of the sauce to a small bowl and whisk in 1 tablespoon cornstarch until smooth. Then, whisk this mixture back into the curry sauce.

Thai Panang Curry with Vegetables

makes 4 servings   prep time: 15 minutes   cook time: 30 minutes

*R*enee sometimes calls Thai Curry "Curry soup."

Optional: 1 batch crispy baked tofu (see recipe on page 115)

Optional: 1 ¼ cups brown jasmine rice or long-grain brown rice, rinsed

1 tablespoon coconut oil or olive oil

1 small white or yellow onion, chopped (about 1 cup)

Pinch of salt, or more, to taste

1 red bell pepper, sliced into thin (¼" wide) strips

1 yellow, orange or green bell pepper, sliced into thin (¼" wide) strips

3 carrots, peeled and sliced on the diagonal into ¼" thick rounds (about 1 cup)

2 cloves garlic, pressed or minced

1 to 2 tablespoons panang curry paste* (use 1 for mild or 2 for spicy)

1 14-ounce can regular coconut milk

½ cup water

2 tablespoons peanut butter

1 tablespoon tamari or soy sauce

1 ½ teaspoons coconut sugar or brown sugar

2 teaspoons fresh lime juice, to taste

Optional garnishes: fresh basil or Thai basil, sriracha or chili garlic sauce for extra spice

1. **Rice:** If you'd like to serve rice with your curry (optional), bring a large pot of water to boil. Add the rinsed rice and continue boiling for 30 minutes, reducing heat as necessary to prevent overflow. Remove from heat, drain the rice and return the rice to pot. Cover and let the rice rest for 10 minutes or longer, until ready to serve. Just before serving, season the rice to taste with salt and fluff it with a fork.

2. **Curry:** warm a large skillet with deep sides over medium heat. Once it's hot, add the oil. Add the onion and a sprinkle of salt and cook, stirring often, until the onion has softened and is turning translucent, about 5 minutes.

3. Add the bell peppers and carrots. Cook until the bell peppers are easily pierced through by a fork (3 to 5 more minutes), stirring occasionally. Add the garlic and curry paste and cook, while stirring, for 1 minute.

4. Add the coconut milk and water, and stir to combine. Bring the mixture to a simmer over medium heat. Reduce heat as necessary to maintain a gentle simmer and cook until the peppers and carrots have softened to your liking, about 5 to 10 minutes, stirring occasionally. If you're adding crispy tofu, stir it in now.

5. Remove the pot from the heat. Stir in the peanut butter, tamari, sugar and lime juice. Add salt, to taste (I usually add a pinch or two). If the curry needs a little more punch, add ½ teaspoon more tamari, or for more acidity, add ½ teaspoon more lime juice.

6. Divide rice and curry into bowls and garnish with fresh basil, if using. If you love spicy curries, serve with sriracha or chili garlic sauce on the side.

Recipe courtesy of Rose Frank – from Cookie and Kate

Food for Thought

You can get Thai Curry paste at any Asian store or online. Our favorite brand is Mai Ploy. You can freeze what you don't use once you open the package. Also, this is the basic method for any Thai curry so try different pastes and different vegetables to make it your own.

Chicken Coconut Kurma- Bombay House Style

makes 8 servings   prep time: 15 minutes   cook time: 1 hour and 20 minutes

We seem to forget to buy yogurt for this recipe often. When we go through to list what we need to buy, we just space that crucial ingredient. One Sunday, Rose went to make it and realized she forgot to buy yogurt. We didn't want to run to the store for plain yogurt and we found we had some vanilla yogurt so we used that to marinate the chicken.....It is NOT the same. Please use only plain yogurt in this recipe!

Marinade:
2 pounds boneless chicken thighs

1 cup plain yogurt

½ teaspoon salt

½ teaspoon coriander

½ teaspoon cayenne/red pepper

½ teaspoon turmeric

1 teaspoon garam masala

1 teaspoon cumin

Sauce:
Olive oil

2 tablespoons butter

3 teaspoons garlic, minced

1 small onion, diced

½ teaspoon ground ginger

½ teaspoon turmeric

½ teaspoon cayenne/red pepper for medium heat (no cayenne for mild, 1-2 teaspoons for hot)

1 teaspoon garam masala

1 teaspoon salt

1 teaspoon ground coriander

2 (8-ounce) cans tomato sauce

1 (15-ounce) can coconut milk (regular size)

4 tablespoons heavy whipping cream

Cilantro

Cashew nuts (about¾ cup)

Golden or standard raisins (about½ cup)

White rice

1. Cut the chicken into 1-inch pieces. Place in a Ziploc bag with all the other marinade ingredients and refrigerate until ready to use (2 to 24 hours).

2. Preheat oven to 350 ° F.

3. Add a little olive oil to a pan over medium high heat. Then add half the marinated chicken.

4. Cook the chicken for 4 to 5 minutes on each side until it is no longer pink in the center, then repeat for the other half of the chicken.

5. Melt the butter in a high-sided pan. Add the garlic and onion and cook for 1 minute.

6. Add the spices: ginger, turmeric, cayenne, garam masala, salt, and coriander. Stir for 1 minute.

7. Stir in tomato sauce, coconut milk, heavy whipping cream and raisins. Bring to a boil. You can add the cashews at this point, but they will get soft instead of remaining crunchy. Place the curry, uncovered, in the preheated oven for 1 hour.

8. Stir in the cashews right at the end. Taste and season accordingly.

9. Garnish with cilantro, cashews and golden raisins. Serve with white rice and garlic naan.

Recipe courtesy of Rose and Anthony Frank

Chefnotes

🎩 The amount of cashews and golden raisins can be purely to taste. We have varying levels of love for the golden raisins at our house. Anthony and Luca LOVE them and can't get enough. Rose could pass and so could Milla. Also, you can use whatever cashews you have on hand. We have used salted, unsalted, whole, and pieces.

Chicken Tikka Masala

makes 4 to 6 servings   prep time: 40 minutes   cook time: 40 minutes

This is one of the first (maybe the actual first) curry that the Franks made. We chose our curry journey with an involved recipe! (Note: use a vegetable chopper for the MANY tomatoes!) The Newton's were visiting us for dinner while in town and we wanted to make this for them. Erin said that she was starting to like spicier foods so we went ahead with this recipe. She was basically crying after a couple of bites, the kids couldn't really eat it, and they needed milk to soothe the burning. I said, "I thought you were liking spicy food?" Erin said that she meant she was starting to handle medium salsa. Now we really tone down the spice when we make curries for others.

Marinade:

1 cup plain yogurt, whisked until smooth

1 tablespoon fresh ginger, grated

3 cloves garlic, pressed or finely minced

1 teaspoon kosher salt

½ teaspoon black pepper, freshly ground

1 pound boneless, skinless chicken thighs, cut into large bite-size chunks

Sauce:

3 tablespoons butter

2 teaspoons olive oil

6 cloves garlic, minced

1 (2-inch) thumb of ginger, peeled and minced

2 Serrano pepper, minced (seeds removed if you don't want it spicy)

2 tablespoons tomato paste

2 teaspoons paprika

1 teaspoon garam masala

8 Roma tomatoes, diced

1½ teaspoons kosher salt

2 cups water

1 tablespoon dried fenugreek leaves, optional

½ cup heavy cream

Fresh cilantro leaves, minced

Serving suggestion: Cooked rice, warm naan bread or crusty bread.

1. **Marinade:** In a large bowl, mix the yogurt, ginger, garlic, 1 teaspoon salt, and 1/2 teaspoon black pepper. Poke chicken with a fork, then add to marinade. Cover with foil and marinate at least 30 minutes, or at most overnight, in the refrigerator.

2. **Sauce:** When you're ready to make the curry, place a large skillet over medium heat, and add the butter and olive oil. When butter has melted, add the garlic, ginger, and Serrano pepper. Saute until lightly browned around the edges.

3. Add the tomato paste and cook until the tomato has darkened in color, about 3 minutes. Add the paprika and garam masala, and saute for about 1 minute to draw out their flavors.

4. Add the tomatoes, salt, and water. Bring to a boil, then turn down the heat to a simmer, and cover. Cook for 20 minutes. Take the pan off the heat, and allow the sauce to cool for 5 minutes.

5. Meanwhile, fire up your broiler, and cover your broiler pan in foil. Pull the chicken thigh chunks out of the marinade and place them on the sheet. Place the chicken under the broiler, and cook about 7 minutes on each side, until charred and cooked through.

6. Note: Don't worry if the chicken is still a little uncooked, but very charred on the outside; you can finish cooking the chicken in the sauce.

7. Pour sauce into a blender or food processor, and process until smooth. Pour back into the pan, and

bring back up to a boil. Add the chicken and fenugreek leaves, if using. Reduce heat to a simmer, and cook, covered, for about 10 minutes.

8. Add cream and stir through. Garnish with minced fresh cilantro if you like, and serve over rice, with naan or crusty bread!

Recipe courtesy of Rose and Anthony Frank – from Food network, Aarti Sequeira

Food for Thought

Wear food safe gloves when you deseed the serranos!

Japanese Curry Roux

3 tablespoons unsalted butter (42 g)

4 tablespoons all-purpose flour (30 g)

1 tablespoon curry powder (6 g)

1 tablespoon garam masala (6 g)

¼ teaspoon cayenne pepper (1-2 g) (optional for spicy)

1. Gather all the ingredients.
2. In a small saucepan, melt the butter over low heat.
3. When the butter is completely melted, add the flour. Stir to combine the butter and flour.
4. Soon the butter and flour fuse and swell. Keep stirring because the roux will easily burn. Cook for 12 to 15 minutes on low heat.
5. After 15 minutes, the roux will turn to light brown color.
6. Add the garam masala, curry powder, and cayenne pepper.
7. Cook and stir for 30 seconds and remove from the heat. Use the curry roux in your curry recipe. Make sure to taste and season with salt after you add the roux to the dish (as the roux is not salted).
8. To Store: If you don't use it immediately, let it cool in an airtight container with lid and store in the refrigerator for a month or freezer for 3 to 4 months.

Recipe courtesy of Anthony Frank – from Just One Cookbook

Chefnotes

You can substitute with gluten free flour.

Japanese Curry

makes 6 servings   prep time: 30 minutes   cook time: 1 hour

The Koevens come over for dinner and games often. I think this is Wilder's favorite thing we ever make. He got the recipe and made a big batch at home and ate it for days.

Freshly ground black pepper

2 carrots

2 onions

1 to 2 potatoes

½ tablespoon ginger

2 cloves garlic

1½ tablespoons neutral-flavored oil (vegetable, canola, etc)

4 cups water (or chicken stock)

1 apple (I used Fuji apple)

1 tablespoon honey

2 teaspoon kosher/sea salt (use half for table salt)

200 grams Japanese curry roux (see recipe on page 164)

1½ tablespoons soy sauce

1 tablespoon ketchup

Soft/hard-boiled egg

Fukujinzuke (red pickled daikon)

1. Gather all the ingredients.
2. Peel and cut the carrot in rolling wedges (Rangiri) and cut the onions in wedges.
3. Cut the potatoes into 1.5 inch pieces and soak in water for 15 minutes to remove excess starch.
4. Grate the ginger and crush the garlic.
5. Heat 1 1/2 tablespoons vegetable oil in a large pot over medium heat and sauté the onions until they become translucent.
6. Add the ginger and garlic.
7. Add the carrot and mix.
8. Add the chicken broth (or water).
9. Bring the stock to boil and skim the scum and fat from the surface of the stock (if meat is included).
10. Peel the apple and coarsely grate it.
11. Add the honey and salt and simmer uncovered for 20 minutes, stirring occasionally.
12. Add the potatoes and cook for 15 minutes, or until the potatoes are tender. Turn off the heat. Meanwhile you can make homemade curry roux.
13. When the potatoes are ready, add the curry.
14. If you are using homemade curry roux, add a ladleful or two of cooking liquid from the stock and mix into the curry paste. Add more cooking liquid if necessary and mix well until it's smooth.
15. Add the roux paste back into the stock in the large pot and stir to combine.
16. Add soy sauce and ketchup. Simmer uncovered on low heat, stirring occasionally, until the curry becomes thick.
17. Serve the curry with Japanese rice on the side and garnish with soft boiled egg and Fukujinzuke. You can store the curry in the refrigerator up to 2 to 3 days and in the freezer for 1 month. Potatoes will change the texture so you can take them out before freezing.

Recipe courtesy of Anthony Frank – from Just One Cookbook

Chefnotes

🍳 We often make this with Tonkatsu (breaded pork loin, recipe on page 194) and leave off the egg.

Malt Barn Corn Dogs

*W*hen we started the Malt Barn around 1980, Mona made this recipe for Corn Dogs and would hand dip them in the oil when someone ordered them so they were fresh. No one does hand dipped corn dogs these days, but they sure were good.

12 hot dogs

12 sticks

Oil for frying

1 cup cornmeal

2 cups instant pancake mix

Evaporated milk

1. Mix together cornmeal and pancake mix, then add evaporated milk until the batter is the appropriate thickness.

2. Pour 2 to 3 inches of oil in a large pot or dutch oven and heat to 350°F over medium heat.

3. Pat hot dogs dry with paper towels and insert sticks.

4. Dip hot dogs into the batter. To make this easy, fill a drinking glass with batter and dip hot dogs in to coat.

5. Drop battered hot dog into the hot oil.

6. Fry 3 minutes or until golden brown.

Recipe courtesy of Sandy Newton

Brion's Quick Easy Dinner

*W*hen I was a teenager, I made this dinner for my family. It's not fancy, but edible. Bekah and Mom both decided they could eat it after I made it.

1 large can of Dinty Moore Beef Stew
1 can of Vienna sausage
1 can of refrigerated flaky dinner rolls

1. Preheat oven to 350 ° F.
2. Add the Dinty Moore Beef Stew to an 8X10 pan and heat till warm.
3. Cut the Vienna sausages in half in the middle, and add to the stew.

4. Break open the Dinner rolls, separate and split in half.

5. Spread the rolls over the stew and cook at 350 ° F for about 15 to 20 minutes, until the rolls look completely done on the top and are cooked all the way through and not doughy on the bottom.

Recipe courtesy of Brion Robinson

Chefnotes

For extra taste or a larger family add a bag of frozen sweet white corn to the dish before heating and add a little cheese to the mixture to suit your taste.

Jo's Easy Cheesy Chicken Enchiladas

*T*hese are Justin's favorite! He asks for it for every birthday and for special meals.

2 cups chicken, cooked and shredded

1 (10.5-ounce) can cream of chicken soup

16 ounces sour cream

2 cups shredded cheese, any variety

1 (4-ounce) can diced chilies

1 (4-ounce) can diced jalapenos, optional

½ teaspoon salt

¼ teaspoon black pepper

10-12 flour tortillas

1. Cook and shred chicken.
2. Preheat oven to 350 ° F.
3. In a large bowl, combine chicken with cream of chicken soup, sour cream, cheese, chilies, jalapenos, salt, and pepper. Mix together.
4. Add about 1/4 cup of the mixture to each tortilla and roll tightly.
5. Place each filled tortilla in a greased 9x13 baking dish.
6. Spread the remaining mixture on top of the tortillas.
7. Optionally, top with shredded cheese for an extra cheesy meal.
8. Cover with foil and bake in preheated oven for 30 to 40 minutes or until hot.
9. Can remove foil the last 10 minutes of baking for a crispier top.

Recipe courtesy of Jo Jacobs

Food for Thought

I often double (or triple) the recipe and freeze the extra for another night.
The enchiladas can also can be made a day in advance and left in the fridge until ready to bake.

Chefnotes

Made by Justin's family for as long as I have known them. After so many years, no one follows a recipe anymore and it is just from memory at this point. So some ingredients may be more or less depending on who makes it and whose memory is best.

White Sauce Chicken Enchiladas

I love these enchiladas because you make your own, super tasty, white sauce instead of using a boring can of cream of chicken soup.

White Sauce:
2½ tablespoons butter

3 tablespoons all-purpose flour

1 cup milk

½ cup sour cream

1 cup chicken broth

½ teaspoon cumin

1 (4-ounce) can green chiles or jalapeños

½ teaspoon salt

½ teaspoon black pepper

Enchiladas:
2½ cups shredded chicken

1 cup frozen corn

½ cup sliced scallions

Salt and pepper

2 cups grated cheese

8 corn or flour tortillas

1. Melt butter in a skillet. Add flour and cook for 1 minute.

2. Add milk and whisk until mixture thickens. Add sour cream and chicken broth. Whisk and cook for 2 minutes. Stir in cumin, chiles, salt, and pepper. Remove from heat.

3. Preheat oven to 350 ° F.

4. In a large bowl, mix together 1/4 cup white sauce, chicken, corn and scallions, 1 cup grated cheese, and salt and pepper to from the filling.

5. Place a little sauce in the bottom of a 9 x 13 baking dish.

6. Warm tortillas in the microwave for 15 seconds.

7. Divide filling between tortillas. Roll up each tortilla and place in the dish.

8. Top with the rest of the sauce and cheese.

9. Bake at 350 ° F for 25 minutes.

Recipe courtesy of Jen Burge

Grandma's Pork Enchiladas

makes about 20 enchiladas

Meat:

3 pounds pork, approximate

Salt and black pepper, to taste

1 large can tomatoes, preferably crushed or diced

1 teaspoon Italian seasoning

2 to 3 teaspoons cumin

1 teaspoon chili powder

3 large cloves of garlic

⅓ cup dried onion flakes or 1 onion, chopped

2 small cans mandarin oranges with juice

2 cups chicken or vegetable broth

Enchiladas:

3 cups cheddar cheese, grated, approximate

Rosarita Enchilada Sauce, red

20 10-inch flour tortillas

1. **Meat:** Place pork in a slow cooker on low. Salt and pepper to taste. Add the remaining ingredients.
2. Cook roughly 6 to 8 hours, till pork falls to pieces. Cool and chop meat.
3. **Enchiladas:** Preheat oven to 350 ° F. Grease 2 9x13 pans (may need a small third pan as well).
4. For each enchilada, place about 1/3 cup of the meat down the middle of a tortilla. Sprinkle with cheese and then spread a full serving spoon of sauce over that. Roll up and lay side by side in the pan.
5. Pour remaining sauce over enchiladas and top with a layer of cheese.
6. Loosely cover with foil to keep enchiladas from browning too soon or too much.
7. Bake at 350 ° F for about 45 minutes, especially if they are cold out of the fridge. Uncover for last 10 minutes of cooking.

Recipe courtesy of Deborah Robinson

Food for Thought

You may also want to try other kinds of cheese besides cheddar. As much or as little as you want.

As each oven is a little different, watch carefully so as to not burn or dry out the enchiladas. These should be moist, gooey enchiladas.

Adjust them however you want, using more or less sauce or cheese.

Chefnotes

☕ I suggest cooking the meat a day or two before assembling and baking the enchiladas. I also suggest tasting the cooked meat to make sure the seasonings are to your liking.

Ben's Grilled Maple Salmon

*Y*ears ago, for Mother's day I made grilled salmon for a large family get together. Everyone loved it. This is my current iteration of that recipe.

⅓ cup real maple syrup

¼ cup soy sauce

1 tablespoon vegetable oil

2 cloves garlic, pressed or finely chopped

Lemon pepper, to taste

½ teaspoon salt

½ teaspoon black pepper, freshly ground

2 to 2½ pounds salmon fillet

1. Stir together all ingredients except salmon. Place salmon in a dish or zipper bag and pour marinade on top, and turn to coat.

2. Marinate in the refrigerator 45 minutes.

3. Heat the grill to medium high heat, about 350 ° F. Oil the grill. Place salmon on the grill. Cook for 2 to 5 minutes depending on thickness. Carefully flip salmon over and continue grilling until salmon is flaky.

Recipe courtesy of Ben Newton – adapted from natashaskitchen.com

Chefnotes

Can also add the juice from half a lemon, if desired.

Boom Boom Fish Tacos

makes 2 servings   prep time: 20 minutes   cook time: 20 minutes   total time: 40 minutes

The pandemic made us eat a lot of food from Home Chef and other home meal kit companies. This is a recipe that we keep making over and over.

6 ounces canola oil

6 small flour tortillas

⅓ cup tempura mix

¼ cup cold water

1 teaspoons Asian garlic and ginger seasoning

1 shallot

4 ounces pineapple chunks

2 ounces boom boom sauce (can buy at store)

2 heads bok choy

1 ounce seasoned rice wine vinegar

12 ounces tilapia fillets

Pinch of salt and black pepper

1. **Prepare Ingredients:** Cut bok choy stems and leaves into 1/4-inch slices keeping stems and leaves separate. Place leaves in mixing bowl with seasoned rice vinegar for at least 5 minutes.

2. Peel and halve shallot. Slice thinly.

3. Drain pineapple and coarsely chop.

4. Pat tilapia dry and cut into 2-inch pieces. Season all over with garlic and ginger seasoning and pinch of salt and pepper

5. **Cook the Filling:** Place a medium non-stick pan over medium high heat and add 1 teaspoon olive oil.

6. Add bok choy stems and shallot to hot pan and stir occasionally until they begin to char, 3-4 minutes

7. Add pineapple and stir occasionally until lightly charred 1-2 minutes.

8. Remove from burner and add to a plate, set aside

9. **Make the Batter:** Wipe pan clean and return to medium high heat, adding the canola oil. Heat 3-5 minutes

10. While oil heats, whisk the tempura and 1/4 cup cold water in a mixing bowl until a thin batter forms, like a pancake batter. If too thick add additional water, 1 tablespoon at a time, until desired consistency is reached.

11. After 3-5 minutes test oil temperature by adding a pinch of batter to it. It should sizzle gently. If it browns immediately turn the heat down and let the oil cool. If it doesn't brown, increase the heat

12. **Fry the Tilapia:** Line a plate with a paper towel. Dip the tilapia pieces in batter coating evenly.

13. Working in batches carefully add tilapia pieces to hot oil and cook until golden brown and pieces reach 145 ° F, about 2 to 3 minutes per side.

14. Transfer cooked pieces to towel lined plate.

15. **Warm Tortillas and Finish Dish:** Wrap tortillas in a damp paper towel and microwave until warm, 30-60 seconds.

16. Place dish on plate, filling tortillas with tilapia and boom boom sauce. Top with filling and garnish with bok choy leaves. Bon appetit!!

Recipe courtesy of Geeta – from Home Chef

Sofia's Spanakopita

makes one 15 by 10 inch pan   prep time: 30 minutes   cook time: 1 hour and 15 minutes

*D*ylan loves this!

1⅓ cup extra-virgin olive oil

4 cloves garlic, minced

4 cups finely chopped leeks (white part only)

4 cups finely chopped shallots or onions

6 (10-ounce) bags fresh spinach, roughly chopped

4 cups chopped scallions

5 cups cubed feta cheese

4 cups ricotta cheese

1 cup grated kefalotyri cheese

5 tablespoons finely chopped fresh dill

4 teaspoons finely chopped fresh mint

4 teaspoons ground black pepper

3 teaspoons nutmeg, freshly grated

4 large eggs

2 cups olive oil, for brushing

1 box number-10 phyllo dough (thicker)

1 box number-7 phyllo dough (thinner)

2 eggs, beaten

1. Preheat the oven to 350°F.
2. Heat the extra-virgin olive oil in large pot over medium heat. Sauté the garlic, leeks and shallots until soft, about 5 minutes. Add the spinach and scallions and cover the pot for a few minutes until spinach has wilted significantly. Uncover and simmer on medium-low heat to allow the liquids to evaporate (be sure not to let spinach mixture to burn). When the majority of the liquids have evaporated, transfer to a large bowl. Mix the feta, ricotta, kefalotiri, dill, mint, pepper, nutmeg and eggs in a large bowl. Gently fold the cheese mixture into the cooled spinach mixture.
3. Brush a 15-by-10-inch rectangular pan with olive oil. Gently place one sheet of number-10 phyllo in the bottom of the pan and brush with olive oil, making sure to coat well. Repeat this step eight times. This creates a nice strong base for serving.
4. Pour in the spinach filling. Use the entire box of number-7 phyllo on top of the spinach, making sure to coat each layer of dough very well with olive oil. Also make sure to tuck in edges of the phyllo around the pan to make it look pretty. Score the pie in appropriate portion sizes. Brush the top with the beaten eggs; this gives it the beautiful golden brown color that is achieved after approximately 1 hour of baking.

Recipe courtesy of Charlene Poulsen – from Sofia Vasiliades, Sip 'N Bite

Food for Thought

Cover the phyllo dough as you are working with a slightly moist kitchen towel to keep it from drying out. Be sure to work quickly.

Hawaiian Haystacks

1 cup (2 sticks) butter or margarine

1½ cups all-purpose flour

1 teaspoon salt

1 quart chicken broth

2 cups milk

2 (10.5-ounce) cans cream of chicken soup

4 to 5 cups cooked chicken, cubed (about one whole chicken or 4 chicken breasts)

Cooked rice

Toppings:

Cheddar cheese, shredded

Green onions

Celery, chopped

Tomatoes, diced

Pineapple chunks

Peanuts

Chow mein noodles

Peas

Water chestnuts

Raisins

Sunflower seeds

Slivered almonds

Coconut

Mandarin oranges

1. In a large saucepan, melt the butter and mix in flour and salt to make a roux. Cook and stir for 2 to 3 minutes.
2. Pour in the chicken broth and milk and mix until creamy.
3. Add in the cream of chicken soup and the cooked chicken and stir to combine.
4. Serve over rice with a variety of toppings with which each person can make their own "haystack."

Recipe courtesy of Sandy Newton

Rose's Lasagna

makes at least 12 servings   prep time: 30 minutes   cook time: 45 minutes

Once I totally forgot to put mozzarella cheese in this lasagna. That was one weird lasagna.

Sauce:
1 medium onion
1 pound ground beef
1 pound Italian sausage
Salt and black pepper, to taste
1 (12-ounce) can tomato paste
2 teaspoons oregano
2 teaspoons basil
1 (28-ounce) can diced tomatoes

Cheese mixture:
2 cups ricotta cheese
½ cup Parmesan cheese
1 large egg
12 ounces mozzarella cheese, shredded
12 ounces lasagna noodles

1. Cook lasagna noodles according to package directions. Once they are cooked, lay them out on clean dish towels so that they don't get stuck together. I wouldn't recommend oven ready lasagna noodles for this recipe.

2. Preheat oven to 350 ° F.

3. Add small amount of olive oil to a pan and sauté the onions until tender. Add the meat and season with salt and pepper. Brown to your liking and drain fat. Make a space in the middle of the pan and add the tomato paste, oregano, and basil. Stir in. Once incorporated, add in the diced tomatoes and let simmer for 20 minutes.

4. While sauce is simmering, prepare the cheese mixture by combining ricotta cheese, Parmesan cheese, and egg. Full fat ricotta gives the best result but part skim will work. (If you use cottage cheese I will haunt you).

5. You are now ready to assemble the lasagna. Put a small amount of sauce on the bottom of the pan to start then add a layer of noodles. (Usually three across but could differ depending on the size of your pan.) Add a layer of the cheese mixture on top of the noodles followed by more sauce and a layer of mozzarella cheese. Repeat process about three to four times or until you run out of noodles. Top with extra mozzarella and Parmesan. Bake in preheated oven for 45 minutes.

Recipe courtesy of Rose Frank

Chefnotes

Seriously, don't let cottage cheese touch my lasagna recipe!

Eggplant Parmesan

When we lived in Hillsborough, North Carolina we had the good fortune to meet, learn from, and become friends with Elder and Sister Yerkes. They were the couple who served at the institute as CES missionaries. I took a class on the Book of Mormon from Sister Yerkes that was for mothers. It was wonderful and became a hinge point in my testimony and the foundation of several beautiful and important friendships.

We invited the Yerkeses to our house for dinner, and when we went to Boston for the summer we stopped in Connecticut to see them and had dinner with them. I love Elder and Sister Yerkes!

One of their services at the institute was to cook lunches for the lessons that took place at noon. They also kept the cookie jar full. I had the pleasure of enjoying some of their cooking. My favorite was this Eggplant Parmesan!

1 eggplant, sliced
1 large egg, beaten
1 tablespoon milk
All-purpose flour
Italian or seasoned bread crumbs
Olive oil, for frying
Spaghetti sauce
Mozzarella cheese
Parmesan cheese

1. If desired, peel the eggplant. Slice the eggplant.

2. In a small bowl, mix egg with milk. Place some flour in a second small bowl, and Italian or seasoned bread crumbs in a third bowl.

3. Dredge each slice by dunking in each of the three bowls to coat with flour, then the egg mixture, and then the bread crumbs.

4. Fry the dredged eggplant in olive oil.

5. Preheat oven to 350° F.

6. In a casserole dish place a layer of spaghetti sauce.

7. Continue adding layers of fried eggplant, spaghetti sauce, mozzarella cheese, and Parmesan cheese until all the eggplant is used, ending with cheese on the top.

8. Bake in preheated oven for 45 minutes. If baking from frozen adjust temp to 325° F and cook longer, being careful not to burn the top cheese. May want to cover with foil, but try to keep the cheese off the foil.

Recipe courtesy of Erin Newton

Food for Thought

Elder and Sister Yerkes suggest that you must try the "eggplant cookies" as they are fried. They are yummy!
Also, the fried slices freeze well as does the assembled casserole.
This is not a quick and easy recipe, but it is worth the effort and fun to do together with others!

Greek Penne and Chicken

makes 4 servings

The Feta is what sells the recipe. My kids love pasta and can heap on the pasta with as little of the sauce as possible.

1 (16-ounce) package penne pasta

1½ tablespoons butter

½ cup chopped red onion

2 cloves garlic, minced

1 pound skinless, boneless chicken breast halves, cut into bite-size pieces

1 (14-ounce) can artichoke hearts in water

1 tomato, chopped

½ cup crumbled feta cheese

3 tablespoons fresh parsley, chopped

2 tablespoons lemon juice

1 teaspoon dried oregano

Salt, to taste

Ground black pepper, to taste

1. In a large pot with boiling salted water cook penne pasta until al dente. Drain.

2. Meanwhile, in a large skillet over medium-high heat melt butter, add onion and garlic and cook for 2 minutes. Add chopped chicken and continue cooking, stirring occasionally until golden brown, about 5 to 6 minutes.

3. Reduce heat to medium- low. Drain and chop artichoke hearts and add them, chopped tomato, feta cheese, fresh parsley, lemon juice, dried oregano, and drained penne pasta to the large skillet. Cook until heated through, about 2 to 3 minutes.

4. Season with salt and ground black pepper. Serve warm.

Recipe courtesy of Amy Trent – adapted from www.allrecipes.com/recipe/11998

Brooklyn Girl's Penne Arrabiata

*M*y kids love pasta. I gotta find a new way to eat it or I'm going to go crazy. This is pretty good.

½ cup olive oil, divided

6 cloves garlic, sliced

1 teaspoon red pepper flakes

1 (28-ounce) can diced tomatoes with garlic and olive oil

½ cup tomato sauce

1 bunch fresh basil, chopped

1 (12-ounce) package dried penne pasta

2 large eggs

2 cups bread crumbs

1 teaspoon garlic powder

1 teaspoon salt

1 teaspoon black pepper

1 pound thin chicken breast cutlets

1. Heat 1/4 cup of olive oil in a large skillet over medium heat. Add the garlic, and saute for a few minutes. Sprinkle in the red pepper flakes, and saute for another minute. Pour in the diced tomatoes and tomato sauce, and add the basil. Simmer for about 20 minutes, stirring occasionally.

2. Meanwhile, bring a large pot of lightly salted water to a boil. Add penne pasta, and cook for 8 minutes, or until tender. Drain.

3. In a small bowl, whisk eggs with a fork. Place bread crumbs in a separate bowl. Stir the garlic powder, salt and pepper into the bread crumbs. Dip chicken cutlets into the egg, then press into the bread crumbs until completely coated.

4. Heat remaining olive oil in a large skillet over medium heat. Fry chicken for about 5 minutes per side, or until the coating is a nice dark brown color.

5. Remove chicken, and cut into slices. Toss the chicken slices into the sauce, and simmer for about 10 minutes. Stir in the cooked penne, and simmer for a few more minutes to soak up the flavor, then serve.

Recipe courtesy of Amy Trent – adapted from www.allrecipes.com/recipe/77758

Butternut Pasta

The first time I tried this, I was taking care of Emma and Libby at the North Carolina house while Sam was being born. Erin left a butternut squash that needed to be used, and gave me the idea for how to use it. Several years and lots of messipes later....this is one of my favorite foods. Wilder asked me to make it for his birthday, and that's how I know it is done.

2 butternut squashes
16 ounces penne pasta
1 pound sausage (preferably sage and fennel)
1½ cups full fat ricotta cheese
Olive oil, salt, black pepper, and sage, to taste

1. Preheat oven to 400 ° F.
2. Cut both squashes in half.
3. **For the top halves with no seeds:** Cut off the peel and the top, then dice into small cubes. Toss with olive oil, salt, pepper, and sage. Spread evenly over a sheet pan and roast at 400 ° F until soft and browned (roughly 35 minutes).
4. **For the bottom halves with seeds:** Cut off the peel and rub the entire half with olive oil. Place each half on a sheet pan and sprinkle with salt and pepper. Roast at 400 ° F until totally soft, at least an hour.
5. Brown the sausage and break into small pieces.
6. Boil the penne until soft, then drain
7. While the solid halves of squash are still roasting, add the pasta, sausage, and diced squash into a large bowl and mix evenly.
8. Add half a cup ricotta cheese and mix with other ingredients. Set aside.
9. When the solid halves of squash are soft, cut into smaller pieces and add to a food processor. Blend until smooth. Add the remaining cup of ricotta cheese, salt, pepper, and sage. Blend.
10. Add the pureed squash to the large bowl of other ingredients and mix together. Pour ingredients into a large baking dish and bake together at 350 ° F until heated through, then serve.

Recipe courtesy of Amy Koeven

Jordan's Tortellini Alfredo

makes 4 servings   prep time: 5 minutes   cook time: 30 minutes   total time: 35 minutes

Brittney and I have a favorite Italian restaurant in Moab with amazing food, especially their alfredo sauce. We eat there every time we go to Moab and it has become a special place for us. This recipe is my best attempt at recreating that amazing alfredo sauce, and, if I do say so myself, I did a pretty good job!

1 (20-ounce) package refrigerated cheese tortellini

½ cup butter

2 cups heavy whipping cream

3 cloves fresh garlic, minced

2½ cups grated Parmesan cheese

1 cup grated mozzarella

½ cup milk

1 teaspoon dried oregano

1 teaspoon ground black pepper

2 teaspoons salt

1. In a large stock pot bring water to a boil for the tortellini. Add the pasta when water has started to boil. Follow the directions on the package for the amount of water and cooking time, typically 7 to 10 minutes. Drain when fully cooked and set aside.

2. Simultaneously, in a large, oven-safe saucepan melt the butter on medium-low heat. After butter is melted add the cream and bring to a simmer, then lower the heat to low and simmer for 3 to 5 minutes, stirring occasionally. Slowly whisk in the garlic, the Parmesan cheese, and 1/2 cups mozzarella (the other half will be used as topping). Let simmer for 10 minutes, stirring occasionally. Sauce may appear thick and gloopy but will smooth out over time. Add the salt, pepper, oregano, and milk. Increase heat to medium low and cook for another 5 minutes.

3. At this point the pasta should have been cooked and drained. Add the cooked pasta directly to the sauce and stir to fully incorporate. Top the dish with the remaining mozzarella and put the saucepan in the oven (double check you pan is oven-safe) under a high broiler for 2-3 minutes until the cheese is melted and begins to brown and bubble. Serve directly from the pan. (If you do not have an oven safe pan you can just keep the mixture on the stove for a few more minutes until the cheese is melted or leave off the cheese topping and serve as is.)

Recipe courtesy of Jordan Poulsen

Food for Thought

Keep it low and slow! The key to this dish is keeping the sauce on a low heat and taking your time to let it do it's thing. Don't rush it or you may end up with a gloopy mess. The best things in life are worth waiting for, right?

Use any pasta you like, tortellini is just what inspired the recipe and is the classic in our house. Ravioli is another great option.

Tortellini will absorb lots of water while it cooks and will swell a lot in the pot. Make sure your pot is large enough and has extra room, and always go bigger if you aren't sure.

Thick-grated mozzarella works best for the cheese topping. It bubbles and browns better for a better texture and appearance. But don't stress if it's not available. Any grated mozzarella will do.

The milk is used to thin out the sauce. If you like a thicker sauce you can omit the milk, or add more milk if you want it even thinner.

No-Cook Pasta Sauce

2 pounds plum tomatoes (about 8 medium tomatoes), chopped

¼ cup chopped fresh basil leaves

2 tablespoons chopped red onions

½ cup Kraft Light House Italian Reduced Fat Dressing

¼ cup Kraft 100% Grated Parmesan or Romano Cheese

1 pound pasta, cooked and drained

1. Combine tomatoes, basil and onions in large bowl.
2. Stir in dressing and cheese.
3. Add pasta and toss lightly.

Recipe courtesy of Rebekah Emerson

Homemade Mac and Cheese

I like to think I am smart, or at least mostly smart. When Justin and I were first married I made this recipe a few times and we liked it those few times. One time we didn't have evaporated milk, so I figured I would use sweetened condensed milk. This was before iPhones and Alexa, when you couldn't just easily pull it up on your phone or ask your favorite assistant to search for appropriate food substitutions. For those smarter than me, you know how this story ends...and for those newly married who think they are familiar with how to cook and bake, well we all make mistakes. Lesson learned, you can be mostly smart and still do silly things. My newly-wed, sweet husband choked down extra sweet, basically candied mac and cheese for as long as he could until I took my first bite and spit it out. Probably one of my most embarrassing moments...most of you know another embarrassing moment of mine involving a shelf, but that's a story for a different book.

16 ounces elbow pasta

4 tablespoons butter

2 large eggs, beaten

1 (6-ounce) can evaporated milk

½ teaspoon salt

½ teaspoon black pepper

½ teaspoon mustard

½ teaspoon hot sauce

8 to 10 ounces sharp or medium cheddar cheese, shredded

1. Whisk together eggs, evaporated milk, salt, pepper, mustard, and hot sauce. Set aside.

2. Cook pasta to al dente and drain. Return to pot with heat on low.

3. Add butter and stir together until melted.

4. Remove pot from heat and slowly add in milk mixture, continually stirring to avoid scrambling the eggs. Mix until pasta is fully coated.

5. Place pot back on low heat and begin to add in shredded cheese, small amounts at a time. As the cheese starts to melt, the heat can be slowly turned up to medium-low and eventually to medium to fully melt cheese.

6. Enjoy!

Recipe courtesy of Jo Jacobs

Food for Thought

DO NOT substitute sweetened condensed milk for evaporated milk!
I recommend using a big pot to allow for easier mixing.

Chefnotes

🍳 Put leftovers in a baking dish. Top with bread crumbs and bake for lunch or dinner the next day.

CHAPTER 11. MAIN DISHES

Mom's Spaghetti Sauce

1½ pounds ground beef
3 (8-ounce) cans tomato sauce
3 cans water
¼ teaspoon garlic powder
¼ teaspoon Italian seasoning
6 tablespoons Parmesan cheese
1 teaspoon salt

⅛ teaspoon chili powder
1 tablespoon white sugar
6 tablespoon parsley
1 (64-ounce) bottle of vegetable juice

1. Brown ground beef.
2. Add the rest of ingredients and simmer till thick.

Recipe courtesy of Rebekah Emerson

Chefnotes

If you instead make meatballs, divide spices in half and mix half with the meat.

Charlene's Spaghetti Sauce

8 cups tomatoes, blanched and peeled
2 cups onions, chopped
2 cloves garlic, chopped
⅓ cup olive oil
1 teaspoon white sugar
1 teaspoon fresh basil
1 tablespoon fresh oregano
1½ teaspoon salt
1 teaspoon fresh rosemary

¼ teaspoon black pepper
2 cups red wine
1 (12-ounce) can of tomato paste

1. Cook down the tomatoes, then add everything else.
2. Cook until it tastes good.
3. Can be canned in a steamer for 30 minutes, the following day. Follow canning instructions for tomato sauce, which can likely be found online.

Recipe courtesy of Charlene Poulsen

Food for Thought

I don't think I ever followed this recipe exactly. I just got all the stuff in it until it tasted good.

Chefnotes

I suppose you could substitute the wine with vinegar, never tried, but you need the acidity for canning.

Bolognese

makes 6 servings   prep time: 30 minutes   cook time: 60 minutes

*T*his is one of Rose's favorites that she wanted while she was pregnant, noodles optional. (Rose will just eat it with a spoon!)

1 tablespoon olive oil

1 pound ground Italian sausage (Or a 50/50 mix with ground beef)

1 carrot, diced

½ yellow onion, diced

3 cloves of garlic, diced or minced

Fresh ground black pepper and salt, to taste

1 cup red cooking wine

1 (28-ounce) can of crushed tomatoes (San Marzano are the best)

1 cup milk

1. In a deep skillet, add olive oil and meat. Cook to brown the meat to your liking.

2. Break up the meat into small chunks, then add the diced carrots and onions and just allow them to sweat.

3. Add the garlic and cook for a short time so that it doesn't burn (A minute or less)

4. Add some fresh ground black pepper and salt to taste.

5. Add the wine and allow to reduce by half.

6. Add crushed tomatoes and milk and combine.

7. Simmer the sauce for around an hour or until you see fat separating out at the edges.

Recipe courtesy of Anthony Frank – Kenji Lopez-alt

Exquisite Pizza Sauce

makes enough for 1 pizza

*K*ids love pizza. Making our own pizza is cheaper than ordering. We started doing Friday Family Movie Night!!! Pizza is easy to eat in front of a silly Disney movie or episode of Sofia the First.

1 (6-ounce) can tomato paste
¾ cup warm water, at 110 degrees
3 tablespoons grated Parmesan cheese
1 teaspoon minced garlic
2 tablespoons honey
1 teaspoon anchovy paste (Optional)
¾ teaspoon onion powder
¼ teaspoon dried oregano
¼ teaspoon dried marjoram
¼ teaspoon dried basil
¼ teaspoon ground black pepper

⅛ teaspoon cayenne pepper
⅛ teaspoon dried red pepper flakes
Salt, to taste

1. In a small bowl, combine tomato paste, water, Parmesan cheese, garlic, honey, anchovy paste, onion powder, oregano, marjoram, basil, ground black pepper, cayenne pepper, red pepper flakes and salt; mix together, breaking up any clumps of cheese.
2. Sauce should sit for 30 minutes to blend flavors; spread over pizza dough and prepare pizza as desired.

Recipe courtesy of Amy Trent – adapted from www.allrecipes.com/recipe/17319

Pork Chop Bake

makes 6 servings

6 pork chops, 1 inch thick
4 medium potatoes, uncooked, peeled, and thinly sliced
1 (4-ounce) can sliced mushrooms, drained
1 cup water
1 (1-ounce) envelope Lipton Onion Soup mix

1. Preheat oven to 350° F. In large skillet, brown pork chops; drain on absorbent paper. In a buttered 2-quart oblong, baking dish, arrange potatoes, mushroom, and chops. In small bowl, combine water and soup mix; pour over meat. Cover with foil and bake 1 1/2 hours or until potatoes are tender.

Recipe courtesy of Becky Robinson

Baked Spare Ribs

3 pounds spare ribs

½ cup ketchup

½ cup white sugar

2 tablespoons soy sauce

1 tablespoon Worcestershire sauce

1 tablespoon vinegar or wine vinegar

1 to 2 tablespoon all-purpose flour

½ teaspoon powdered ginger

1 teaspoon salt

1 clove garlic, minced

1. Preheat oven to 350° F.

2. Cut the spare ribs into pieces and set aside.

3. In a medium bowl, mix together remaining ingredients.

4. Dip spare ribs in the sauce to coat them and then place in a 9x13 baking dish.

5. Pour remaining sauce over the top of the ribs.

6. Bake in preheated oven for 1 hour, then turn down the heat to 300° F and bake for another hour. Skim off any fat before serving.

Recipe courtesy of Sherry Poulsen and Sandy Newton

Food for Thought

Sherry uses 2 tablespoons of flour, whereas Sandy's recipe only called for 1 tablespoon.

Bama's Ham Stuffed Potatoes
makes 6 stuffed potatoes

*W*hen Dave and I got married someone gave us a cookbook that was good meals on a budget. One day I decided to make this recipe and it was wonderful. I have used it for many guest dinners and it is a favorite of our family, especially Stacy.

6 large potatoes

1 medium chopped onion

½ cup chopped celery

2 tablespoons margarine

2 cups cooked ham, diced

¼ to ½ teaspoon garlic powder

¼ teaspoon salt

¼ cup margarine, melted

¼ cup all-purpose flour

2 cups milk

Breadcrumbs or cheese, optional

1. Bake potatoes at 450 ° F for 45 to 60 minutes.
2. Remove potatoes from oven and cut each in half lengthwise.
3. Scoop out insides from potato shells into a medium bowl. Set aside potato shells for use later.
4. In a saucepan cook celery, onion in butter until tender.
5. Add ham, garlic powder, and salt to vegetables. Cover and simmer for 10 minutes.
6. In a large pot melt margarine. Whisk in flour until smooth.
7. Add milk a little at a time while whisking until smooth after each addition. Cook until thick and bubbly.
8. Add ham mixture and potatoes to the cream sauce and stir to combine.
9. Spoon the potato mixture into the potato shells and place them on a baking sheet.
10. Sprinkle breadcrumbs or cheese on top, if desired.
11. Bake at 350 ° F for 30 minutes.

Recipe courtesy of Sandy Newton

Dinner in a Pumpkin

makes 6 servings   prep time: 25 minutes   cook time: 1 hour 15 minutes

1 medium pumpkin (make sure it will fit in your oven)

1 tablespoon olive oil

2 cups chopped assorted vegetables such as celery, carrots, onions, green peppers, sweet potatoes, potatoes, and mushrooms

1 pound lean ground turkey

1 tablespoon soy sauce

1 (10.5-ounce) can condensed cream of chicken soup

2 cups prepared brown rice

1. Cut off the top of the pumpkin and thoroughly clean out the pulp and seeds.

2. Preheat the oven to 350° F.

3. Add oil in a large skillet over medium heat.

4. Add assorted vegetables and sauté until tender.

5. Add meat, breaking up into small pieces and cook until browned

6. Stir in soy sauce and cooked brown rice. Mix well

7. Pour meat and vegetable mixture into the cleaned pumpkin.

8. Replace pumpkin top and place entire pumpkin on a baking sheet.

9. Cook for 1 hour or until inside meat of the pumpkin is tender.

Recipe courtesy of Libby Newton – adapted from Six Sisters' Stuff

Chefnotes

While you're scooping out the yummy dinner, don't forget to scrape off some of the inside of the pumpkin to eat with it. It tastes just like spaghetti squash.

Frozen Vegetable Stir-Fry

makes 6 servings

2 tablespoons soy sauce

1 tablespoon brown sugar

2 teaspoons garlic powder

2 teaspoons peanut butter

2 teaspoons olive oil

1 (16-ounce) package frozen mixed vegetables

1. Combine soy sauce, brown sugar, garlic powder, and peanut butter in a small bowl.

2. Heat oil in a large skillet over medium heat; cook and stir frozen vegetables until just tender, 5 to 7 minutes. Remove from heat and fold in soy sauce mixture.

Recipe courtesy of Amy Trent – adapted from www.allrecipes.com/recipe/222658

Korean Beef and Rice

South Korea is where I served my mission, but I didn't pick up many cooking skills while I was there. Milla introduced me to this recipe that she learned from Rose. LOVE IT! Every time I make this Eleanor tells me she hates it, until she finally takes a bite and remembers it's awesome! Wrap the Bulgogi and rice in seaweed or a lettuce leaf if you want something fun.

1 pound lean ground beef

3 garlic cloves, minced

1 tablespoon sesame oil

½ cup brown sugar

¼ cup soy sauce

¼ teaspoon ground ginger

Salt and black pepper, to taste

1 teaspoon crushed red pepper flakes (more or less depending on how spicy you like it)

Cooked rice

1 bunch green onions, diced

1. Heat a large skillet over medium heat and brown beef with garlic in the sesame oil.

2. Drain most of the fat and add brown sugar, soy sauce, ginger, salt, pepper and red peppers.

3. Simmer for a few minutes to blend the flavors.

4. Serve over steamed rice and top with green onions.

Recipe courtesy of Amy Trent – adapted from www.sixsistersstuff.com/recipe/korean-beef-and-rice

Food for Thought

You can add vegetables to the meat when you add the sauce. We (the royal we) like broccoli, green beans, bell peppers, and carrots.

Asian Lettuce Wraps

makes 4 servings

This recipe has been a family favorite for several years. It's just like lettuce wraps you would find at a fancy Asian restaurant, but in my opinion my recipe is better.

1 head iceberg lettuce

1 pound ground beef or ground turkey

1 tablespoon vegetable oil

1 large onion, chopped

2 cloves garlic, minced

2 tablespoons soy sauce

½ cup hoisin sauce

2 teaspoons minced pickled ginger or dried ground ginger

2 tablespoons rice wine vinegar

Asian chili pepper sauce, to taste, if desired

1 (8-ounce) can water chestnuts, drained and finely chopped

2 teaspoons Asian sesame oil

1. Slice lettuce into extra large pieces as if to make a bowl out of them, rinse, pat dry and set aside.

2. In a medium skillet over high heat, brown the ground meat in the cooking oil, stirring often and reducing the heat to medium if needed. Drain and set aside in a separate dish to cool.

3. In the same pan, cook the onion until translucent. Add the garlic, soy sauce, hoisin sauce, ginger, vinegar, and chili pepper sauce to the onions, and stir. Stir in the water chestnuts, green onions, sesame oil, and cooked meat. Continue cooking until the green onions just begin to wilt.

4. To serve, allow each person to spoon a portion of the meat into a lettuce leaf. Wrap the lettuce around the meat like a burrito, and enjoy!

Recipe courtesy of Jen Burge

Chefnotes

I prefer using ground turkey in this recipe instead of ground beef.

Gyoza

makes 6 to 8 servings   total time: 60 minutes

When Anthony and I first started making gyoza we would make about 200 at a time. It took hours to wrap them all. Once we invited some deaf friends over to make gyoza since they also loved Japanese food. That was a silly idea considering we needed our hands to talk and to wrap the gyoza! Whoops.

We have tried several recipes and even made some up. This is our current favorite.

Dumplings:

1 pound finely minced Napa cabbage (about½ a medium head)

1 tablespoon kosher salt, divided

1 pound ground pork shoulder

1 teaspoon white pepper

1 tablespoon minced fresh garlic (about 3 medium cloves)

1 teaspoon minced fresh ginger

2 ounces minced scallions (about 3 whole scallions)

2 teaspoons white sugar

1 package dumpling wrappers (40 to 50 wrappers)

Vegetable or canola oil for cooking

Sauce:

½ cup rice vinegar

¼ cup soy sauce

2 tablespoons chili oil (optional)

1. **For the Dumplings:** Combine cabbage and 2 teaspoons salt in a large bowl and toss to combine. Transfer to a fine mesh strainer and set it over the bowl. Let stand at room temperature for 15 minutes.

2. Transfer cabbage to the center of a clean dish towel and gather up the edges. Twist the towel to squeeze the cabbage, wringing out as much excess moisture as possible. Discard the liquid.

3. Combine pork, drained cabbage, remaining teaspoon salt, white pepper, garlic, ginger, scallions, and sugar in a large bowl and knead and turn with clean hands until the mixture is homogeneous and starting to feel tacky/sticky. Transfer a teaspoon-sized amount to a microwave-safe plate and microwave on high power until cooked through, about 10 seconds. Taste and adjust seasoning with more salt, white pepper, and/or sugar if desired.

4. Set up a workstation with a small bowl of water, a clean dish towel for wiping your fingers, a bowl with the dumpling filling, a parchment-lined rimmed baking sheet for the finished dumplings, and a stack of dumpling wrappers covered in plastic wrap.

5. To form dumplings, hold one wrapper on top of a flat hand. Using a spoon, place a 2 teaspoon- to 1 tablespoon-sized amount of filling in the center of the wrapper. Use the tip of the finger on your other hand to very gently moisten the edge of the wrapper with water (do not use too much water). Wipe fingertip dry on kitchen towel.

6. Working from one side, carefully seal the filling inside the wrapper by folding it into a crescent shape, pleating in edge as it meets the other (see here for more detailed step by step instructions). Transfer finished dumplings to the parchment lined baking sheet.

7. At this point the dumplings may be frozen by placing the baking sheet in the freezer. Freeze dumplings for at least 30 minutes then transfer to a zipper-lock freezer bag for long-term storage. Dumplings can be frozen for up to 2 months and cooked directly from the freezer.

8. **To Cook:** Heat 1 tablespoon of vegetable oil in a medium non-stick skillet over medium heat until

shimmering. Add as many dumplings as will fit in a single layer and cook, swirling pan, until evenly golden brown on the bottom surface, about 1 1/2 minutes.

9. Increase heat to medium-high, add 1/2 cup of water and cover tightly with a lid. Let dumplings steam for 3 minutes (5 minutes if frozen), then remove lid. Continue cooking, swirling pan frequently and using a thin spatula to gently dislodge the dumplings if they've stuck to the bottom of the pan, until the water has fully evaporated and the dumplings have crisped again, about 2 minutes longer. Slide dumplings onto a plate, turning them crisped-side-up before serving with the sauce.

10. **For the Sauce:** Combine vinegar, soy sauce, and chili oil.

Recipe courtesy of Anthony Frank – from Serious Eats

Chefnotes

☞ Rose Prefers regular cabbage to napa so if that is what you have it will work just fine.
Also, squeezing the liquid out of the cabbage may seem unnecessary but it really makes a difference.
Often listed as an appetizer in Japanese cookbooks, but we usually eat it as a main dish.

Tonkatsu

makes 2 servings   prep time: 15 minutes   cook time: 15 minutes   total time: 30 minutes

2 boneless pork loin chops (½ inch thick) (thickness: 1-1.3 cm, about ½ inch; weight: 100 g, 3.5 oz each piece)

½ teaspoons kosher/sea salt

⅛ teaspoons freshly ground black pepper

3 cups neutral-flavored oil (vegetable, rice bran, canola, etc) (for deep frying; Recommend 1 ¾ – 2 inch (5 cm) oil in a pot)

Tonkatsu Breading:

2 tablespoons all-purpose flour

1 large egg (50 g w/o shell)

½ tablespoons neutral-flavored oil (vegetable, rice bran, canola, etc) (for egg)

½ cup panko (Japanese breadcrumbs) (You may need more panko depending on the brand)

For Serving:

¼ cabbage (optional; tonkatsu is typically served with shredded cabbage)

1 Persian/Japanese cucumber

2 tablespoons Japanese sesame dressing (for my homemade recipe, click here)

Sesame Tonkatsu Sauce:

1 tablespoons toasted white sesame seeds (optional)

1 tablespoons toasted black sesame seeds (optional)

4 tablespoons tonkatsu sauce (for drizzling over tonkatsu)

1. **Gather all the ingredients:** For Tonkatsu, I highly recommend getting fresh panko (we call it "Nama Panko") from a Japanese grocery store. If you can't get it, follow my instructions to make the fresh panko. Make sure to use a Japanese brand of panko from Japan. Western "panko breadcrumbs" are a bit different from Japanese ones.

2. **To Prepare Shredded Cabbage (Optional):** You can always cut the cabbage super thinly with a sharp knife, but I love this cabbage slicer and it saves time and energy! I also thinly slice the cucumber diagonally, then cut them into thin strips. Toss the cabbage and cucumber together and set aside.

3. **To Make Sesame Tonkatsu Dipping Sauce (Optional):** Grind white and black toasted sesame seeds in Japanese pestle and mortar. Leave some unground for the texture.

4. In individual small plates/bowls, serve 1 tablespoon of the ground sesame seeds and add Tonkatsu sauce. Each person can mix together when they are ready to eat.

5. **To Make Fresh Panko:** Put the panko in a deep dish and spray water until the panko is moist (I use this mister for my pants, too, and love it). Set aside for 15 minutes, or until the panko becomes soft and tender. You can also use a food processor to make fresh panko from Shokupan (Japanese Pullman bread).

6. **To Prepare Pork:** With a sharp knife, remove the extra fat and make several slits on the connective tissue (white area) between the meat and fat. The reason why you do this is that red meat and fat have a different elasticity, and when they are cooked, they will shrink and expand at different rates. This will allow Tonkatsu to stay nice and flat when deep frying and prevent it from curling up.

7. Flip the meat and make several slits on the other side of the connective tissue.

8. Pound both sides of the meat with the back of a knife or a meat tenderizer/pounder.

9. Mold the meat back into its original shape with your hands.

10. Season both sides of the meat with salt and pepper

11. **To Bread the Pork:** Crack the egg in a deep dish and add oil. Whisk together until well combined. By adding oil, the meat and breading won't detach from each other while deep frying and the juice

and flavor from the meat will not escape easily. Prepare a deep dish for flour, too.

12. Dredge the pork in flour and dust off any excess flour. Excess flour will create a coating that prevents the egg mixture from latching onto the pork. Then dip the pork in the egg mixture and coat nicely.

13. Dredge the pork in panko and remove excess panko while pressing down the panko gently. While deep frying, panko will "pop up" so at this moment they don't have to be fluffy. Set aside for 5-10 minutes so the meat and breading will be set.

14. Add oil to the pot and bring it to 340 ° F over medium heat. If you don't have a thermometer, stick a chopstick in the oil and see if tiny bubbles start to appear around the tip of the chopstick. Alternatively, you can drop one piece of panko into the oil, and if it sinks down to the middle of oil and immediately comes right up, then the oil is ready.

15. Gently put one pork into the oil and cook for 1 minute (without flipping). Don't touch the pork for 30 seconds. Why one piece? You don't want to reduce the oil temperature drastically. The size of the bubbles should be big when you add the pork. Keep watching the oil temperature and make sure it doesn't go over 340 ° F or else the panko gets too dark and the pork is undercooked.

16. After a minute, flip the pork and cook the other side for 1 minute.

17. Take out the pork and remove excess oil by holding it vertically for a few seconds. Place on the wire rack or paper towel and let it sit for 4 minutes. The hot oil on the exterior is slowly cooking the meat as it sits.

18. Turn off the heat temporarily and scoop up fried crumbs in the oil with a fine-mesh strainer. It's very important to keep the oil clean (crumbs free) so the oil does not get darker/dirtier with burnt crumbs. Turn on the heat and bring the oil back to 340 ° F.

19. While the first tonkatsu is resting on the wire rack, deep fry the second pork for 1 minute without flipping. Remember not to touch for 30 seconds.

20. Flip and cook the other side for 1 minute.

21. Take out the pork and remove excess oil. Place on the wire rack and let the remaining heat cook for 4 minutes. Scoop up the fried crumbs in the oil with a fine-mesh strainer.

22. The first pork should be ready for the second frying. Bring the oil to 355ºF and fry the pork for 30 seconds on each side.

23. Continue with the second piece of the pork. Drain the oil on the wire rack/paper towel for 2 minutes in a vertical position so the panko does not get soggy on one side.

24. **To Serve:** Cut the tonkatsu into ¾ inch (2 cm) wide pieces.

25. Transfer to a plate and serve it with the shredded cabbage and sesame dressing and the sesame tonkatsu sauce you've prepared.

Recipe courtesy of Rose Frank – Just One Cookbook

Baked Ham and Cheese Party Sandwiches

makes 24 sandwiches

I love the Worcestershire sauce.

¾ cup butter, melted
1½ tablespoons Dijon mustard
1½ teaspoons Worcestershire sauce
1½ tablespoons poppy seeds
1 tablespoon dried minced onion
24 mini sandwich rolls
1 pound thinly sliced cooked deli ham
1 pound thinly sliced Swiss cheese

1. Preheat oven to 350 ° F. Grease a 9x13-inch baking dish.
2. In a bowl, mix together butter, Dijon mustard, Worcestershire sauce, poppy seeds, and dried onion. Separate the tops from bottoms of the rolls, and place the bottom pieces into the prepared baking dish. Layer about half the ham onto the rolls. Arrange the Swiss cheese over the ham, and top with remaining ham slices in a layer. Place the tops of the rolls onto the sandwiches. Pour the mustard mixture evenly over the rolls.
3. Bake in preheated oven until the rolls are lightly browned and the cheese has melted, about 20 minutes. Slice into individual rolls through the ham and cheese layers to serve.

Recipe courtesy of Amy Trent – adapted from www.allrecipes.com/recipe/216756

Dave Newton's Spam Delight

*T*his easy recipe is one of Papa Dave's quick meal treats. Spam?? Really? Yep. Give it a try.....you might even like it!!!

6 tablespoons (¾ stick) butter

1 cup brown sugar

1 (12-ounce) can SPAM

4 to 5 cups real mashed potatoes or instant potatoes mixed to a firm consistency.

Bread crumbs

Melted butter

1. Preheat oven to 350 ° F.
2. In a small saucepan, melt butter.
3. Add brown sugar and mix.
4. Spread brown sugar mixture evenly on the bottom a 9x13 glass baking dish.
5. Cut spam into 1/4 inch slices and layer on top of the brown sugar mixture.
6. Spoon mashed potatoes over spam slices.
7. Top with bread crumbs that have been mixed with melted butter.
8. Bake in preheated oven for 20 minutes or until top is golden brown.

Recipe courtesy of Dave Newton

Food for Thought

Ham slices can be used instead of spam, if so desired.

Cabbage Stew and Dumplings
makes 4 to 6 servings

1 pound ground beef

2 medium onions, thinly sliced

1½ cup coarsely chopped cabbage

½ cup chopped celery

1 (15 to 16-ounce) can kidney beans, with liquid

1 cup water

1 teaspoon salt

¼ teaspoon black pepper

1 to 2 tablespoons chili powder

2¼ cup Bisquick baking mix (or similar)

⅔ cup milk

1. Cook ground beef in a stock pot or dutch oven until brown.

2. Add onions, cabbage, and celery to the meat and cook until vegetables are light brown.

3. Stir kidney beans, water, salt, pepper, and chili powder into mixture.

4. Heat to boiling, then reduce heat.

5. Mix together the baking mix and milk to form a soft dough.

6. Drop the sticky dough by spoonfuls into the boiling stew.

7. Cook uncovered 10 minutes and then covered for an additional 10 minutes, being careful not to burn the stew.

Recipe courtesy of Sandy Newton

Sandy's Beef Stroganoff

This recipe is fun and easy because it is all made up in one skillet.

1 pound ground beef

¾ teaspoon salt

¼ teaspoon black pepper

2 tablespoons minced onion

2 cups water

2 cups egg noodles

1 (10-ounce) can cream of chicken soup

½ cup sour cream

2 teaspoons chopped chives

1. In a fry pan or saute pan cook ground beef, salt, pepper, and onion until meat browns.

2. Add water and noodles and cook until noodles are tender. (may need extra water)

3. Just before serving, mix in cream of chicken soup and sour cream, and top with chives.

Recipe courtesy of Sandy Newton

Hamburger Stroganoff

makes 4 to 6 servings

4 tablespoons (½ stick) butter

½ cup minced onion

1 clove garlic, minced

1 pound ground beef

2 tablespoons all-purpose flour

1 teaspoon salt

¼ teaspoon black pepper

1 pound fresh or 1 8-ounce can sliced
  mushrooms

1 (10.5-ounce) can cream of chicken soup,
undiluted

1 cup sour cream

Parsley

1. Melt butter in a pan. Sauté onion and minced garlic in the butter. Stir in the meat and brown. Stir in flour, salt, pepper, and mushrooms. Cook for 5 minutes. Stir in soup and simmer uncovered 10 minutes. Stir in the sour cream. Heat through. Serve over rice or noodles, if desired. Garnish with parsley.

Recipe courtesy of Becky Robinson – from Betty Crocker's "Dinner for Two Cookbook"

Chefnotes

☞ You might want to use less butter if the hamburger is not lean.

Chapter 12

Turkey

TURKEY IN TROUBLE

CHAPTER 1 - THINKING

I hurd I was going to get eatin for thancksgiving. I started thinking about a dusgise so I wouldn't get eatin. I started thinking about what safe things and Dusgises. I dusided to do more then one dusgise. The dusgise I dusided to do was a Monster Ninga.

CHAPTER 2 - BIULDING

I was geting ready for biulding and makeing stuff. First I went back in the house and got out the book that tell's you how to make wepin's. The first thing I needed to do was going to find some rocks. Next on the list it said put all the rock's in a big pot and put any licwid in and stur it so thats what I did. next on the list it said get any metal then get that licwid and make them tuch. then think wat you want it to turn into and it will happen. I made a sword, a shield, and some armor.

CHAPTER 3 - THE TALK

I went outside. my turkey wife was like what are you doing! and I was like What do you think I'm doing well if you want to know what I'm doing then here's your answer. I'm hiding no, I mean I'm waiting for them t...Who's them. the people who want to kill me but don't worrei I won't die.

CHAPTER 5 - THE FIGHT

here they come I said oh boy I said. there are more then I expected. I gess I have to fight. When they came they sourounded me. There were animale enimese and even a animale Boss. I quickly killed all the enimes but the boss wasn't easy. in fact it almost killed me. this is how the battle went. the boss was a cow. you know that thing under cows with that he could do any attack that didn't roquire wepins. I dogged all the first attacs but avenjelly he almost sta on me. I just darly dogg that an then I had my chance to kill him so I got him

CHAPTER 6 - THE ESCAPE

that guy was so mad he started chaseing me. I used my adilety that makes me ivisible until I play attack. he gave up chaseing me and I was finlly safe. the end

Luca Frank - age 6

Charlene's Turkey's Finest Hour

makes not enough!   cook time: 20 to 25 minutes

This is a great recipe to use up leftover turkey and is ever so good!

1 can cream of mushroom soup
3 cups cooked turkey
1 cup chopped celery
½ cup slivered almonds
½ cup mayonnaise
1 tablespoon lemon juice
3 boiled eggs, diced
3 tablespoons pimentos
2 teaspoons minced onion
½ teaspoon salt
½ teaspoon black pepper
Topping:

½ cup all-purpose flour
1 cup sesame seeds
½ cup cheddar cheese, grated
¼ teaspoon salt
¼ cup butter, melted

1. Preheat oven to 375 ° F.
2. In a large bowl mix cream of mushroom soup, turkey, celery, almonds, mayonnaise, lemon juice, egg, pimentos, onion, salt and pepper. Transfer to a greased baking dish.
3. Mix remaining ingredients, and spread on top.
4. Bake in preheated oven for 20 to 25 minutes or till it starts bubbling

Recipe courtesy of Charlene Poulsen – from The Salt Lake City Tribune

Chefnotes

Rick loves this!

Turkey Vegetable Soup
makes a big batch of good soup

M ake this soup immediately after carving the meat from carcass. Do not let the meat remain on the bone for more than 24 hours before the boil. I've not made it with the noodles, only veggies.

1 leftover whole roasted turkey carcass

2 medium onions, cored, peeled, and chopped

3 medium carrots, peeled and chopped

3 medium stalks celery, cleaned and chopped

2 bay leaves

Salt, to flavor

Freshly ground black pepper

Water, to cover

Leftover turkey meat, diced

2 cups cooked, diced potatoes, rice or pasta

2 cups cooked sweet peas

2 cups cooked carrots, diced

2 cups any other cooked vegetables

2 cloves garlic, chopped

1 cup cooked macaroni

1 cup green onions, chopped, green part only

¼ cup chiffonade fresh basil

¼ cup finely chopped fresh parsley leaves

1 loaf of crusty bread

1. Place turkey carcass in a large stockpot. Add 1/2 of the onions, carrots, and celery. Add bay leaves, salt and pepper. Cover the turkey with 3 quarts of water. Place over medium heat and bring to a boil. Reduce heat to medium low and simmer for 1 hour.

2. Remove stock from heat and strain through a fine mesh sieve, saving the liquid (about 2 quarts) and turkey meat, discarding the vegetables.

3. Sauté remaining onions, carrots, and celery until wilted, about 4 minutes. Add to strained stock. Add the remaining vegetables, and garlic to the stock. Season with salt and pepper. Simmer for 10 minutes. Remove the meat from the turkey carcass and dice. Add the meat, herbs, and cooked macaroni to stock. Heat through.

4. Ladle the soup into each serving bowl and serve with the crusty bread.

Recipe courtesy of Rick Poulsen – from Food Network

Smoked Turkey

*B*ecause I loved Rick's smoked turkey so much, each year at thanksgiving, I've tried to smoke my own turkeys a couple of times. I've adapted this recipe to work for a whole turkey even though it originally only called for a small turkey breast.

1 (64-ounce) bottle apple cider
¾ cup salt
½ cup white sugar
¼ cup apple cider vinegar
3 (4-inch) fresh thyme sprigs
2 (4-inch) fresh rosemary sprigs
10 fresh sage leaves
1 garlic bulb, cut in half crosswise
4 cups ice cubes
1 bone-in turkey breast or whole turkey
Hickory or other types of wood chips

1. Bring cider, salt, sugar, vinegar, thyme, rosemary, sage and garlic to a boil in a large stockpot or 8-quart Dutch oven over medium-high heat; reduce heat to medium, and simmer, stirring occasionally for 5 minutes.

2. Remove from heat and stir in ice cubes. Allow to cool completely, about 1 hour.

3. Place turkey in brine. Cover and chill for 5 to 12 hours.

4. Prepare smoker according to manufacturer's directions, bringing the internal temperature to 225 to 250 ° F; maintain temperature 15 to 20 minutes.

5. Place wood chunks on coals or in smoker.

6. Remove turkey from brine, and pat dry with paper towels. Discard brine. Smoke turkey, maintaining temperature inside smoker between 225 ° F and 250 ° F, until a meat thermometer inserted into thickest portion registers 165 ° F.

7. Remove turkey, and let stand 10 to 15 minutes before slicing.

Recipe courtesy of Ben Newton – from www.southernliving.com/recipes/smoked-turkey-breast

Food for Thought

Recently I used Rick's recipe for the turkey brine, and I think his is easier and better, but here are some of my tips for smoking a turkey, in general. For an 18 pound turkey I ended up needing two batches of Rick's brine. I let it soak in the brine overnight for 7 hours. I started smoking the turkey at 7 a.m. to eat at 4 p.m. I'm always surprised how long it takes to heat up the last few degrees, so make sure you leave yourself plenty of time. I cut up an onion and apple and a few cloves of garlic and put them in the raw turkey cavity to give it more flavor.

I use an upright propane smoker for this recipe and Rick's, and place some of the brine liquid and spices in the liquid pan at the bottom of the smoker, and also add apple juice/cider there as it dries out. I also add soaked wood chips several times (5 or 6 wood chips every 30 minutes to an hour) during the smoking. In my experience, an 18 pound turkey takes 8 to 9 hours to smoke when keeping the temperature around 225 to 250 degrees. I strongly recommend using an electric meat thermometer with a long probe to monitor the temperature of the turkey from outside the smoker. Resist the urge to open the smoker and check on the turkey while it cooks. This will cool off the chamber and the turkey, and lengthen the smoking time.

Rick's Hickory Smoked Turkey

prep time: 2 hours to brine   cook time: 2 to 3 hours

I found this recipe in a Sunset Magazine dated November 1998. This was the first time we as a family sampled it. According to my journal, we had TG dinner at Mona's. In attendance that day was Mom, Dave, Sandy, Stacy, June, Char and Dylan. later that evening we were joined by Gary, Sherry and the kids. It was partly cloudy, windy and mild 60s and 50s.

1 15-20 pound turkey

3 quarts water

1 cup brown sugar, firmly packed

¾ cup salt

1 tablespoon garlic, minced

1 teaspoon black peppercorns

2 dried bay leaves

2 to 3 quarts hot water

2 to 3 cups hickory wood chips

1. Remove and discard leg truss from turkey. Pull off and discard lumps of fat. Remove giblets and neck (reserve for other uses). Rinse bird well.

2. In a bowl or pan (at least 12 to 14 quarts) combine 3 quarts water, brown sugar, salt, garlic, peppercorns, and bay leaves. Stir until sugar and salt are dissolved. Add turkey, cover, and chill for 2 hours, turning bird over occasionally.

3. In a bowl, combine wood chips and 2 to 3 quarts hot water.

4. Lift turkey from brine and rinse thoroughly under cold running water, rubbing gently to release salt; pat dry with towels. Discard brine. Insert a meat thermometer straight down through the thickest part of the turkey breast to the bone.

5. **On a charcoal barbecue:** (20 to 22 inches wide) with a lid, mound and ignite 40 charcoal briquets on firegrate. After about 20 minutes, when coals are spotted with gray ash, push equal portions to opposite sides of firegrate. Place a foil drip pan between mounds of coals. To each mound add 5 briquets and 1/2 cup drained soaked wood chips now and every 30 minutes (until all chips are used). Set grill in place. Set turkey, breast up, on grill over drip pan. Cover barbecue and open vents.

6. **On a gas barbecue:** (with at least 11 inches between indirect-heat burners), place 1 cup drained soaked wood chips in the metal smoking box or in a foil pan directly on heat in a corner. Turn heat to high, close lid, and heat for about 30 minutes. Adjust gas for indirect cooking (heat parallel to sides of bird and not beneath) and set a metal or foil drip pan in center (not over direct heat). Set grill in place. Set turkey, breast up on grill over drip pan. Close barbecue lid. Add another cup of wood chips (sprinkle through or lift grill) every 30 minutes until all are used. If edges of turkey close to heat begin to get too dark, slide folded strips of foil between bird and grill. Fat in drippings may flare when barbecue lid is opened; quench by pouring a little water into the pan.

7. Cook turkey until thermometer registers 160 ° F, likely after 2 to 3 hours, but start checking after 1 hour.

8. Drain juices from cavity into drippings and reserve for other uses. Transfer turkey to a large platter, let rest 15 to 30 minutes before carving.

Recipe courtesy of Rick Poulsen – from Sunset Mag. November 1998

☞ You can brine the bird the day before, then rinse well, cover, and refrigerate until time to cook. It can also brine for a longer time, lately I do 12 hours.

Hickory wood chips are sold beside charcoal briquets.

Chapter 13

Cakes

W HAT BIRTHDAY CAKE would be complete without the singing the "extra" birthday song

We wish a happy, happy, birthday to you!
We wish a happy, happy, birthday to you!
....and when you blow the candles

ou..t,

then all of us will shout
a happy, happy birthday,
a happy, happy birhtday,
a happy, happy birthday to you-u!

Banana Cake

2⅓ cups all-purpose flour
1⅔ cups white sugar
1¼ cups mashed bananas
⅔ cup butter, softened
⅔ cup buttermilk
1¼ teaspoon baking powder
1¼ teaspoon baking soda
¾ teaspoon salt
3 large eggs
Frosting:
3 cups powdered sugar

⅓ cup butter
1½ teaspoons vanilla extract
2 tablespoons milk

1. Preheat oven to 350° F and grease a 9x13 cake pan.

2. Combine all the cake ingredients and mix until well blended.

3. Pour mixture into prepared baking pan and bake in preheated oven for 30 to 40 minutes.

4. Make frosting and frost cake while warm or after it has cooled.

Recipe courtesy of Sherry Poulsen

Cake Devine

This recipe came from an old neighbor of ours, Colleen Huber. This is one of those recipes that is easy to do, looks great and tastes wonderful. Good one to use with large gatherings.

1 (15-ounce) package yellow cake mix

1 package vanilla instant pudding (about 3.4 ounces)

1 cup milk

1 (8-ounce) package of cream cheese, softened

1 (8-ounce) container of Cool Whip

1 (15.5-ounce) can crushed pineapple

1 cup toasted coconut

½ cup maraschino cherries

1. Preheat oven to 350 ° F.
2. Prepare cake mix according to box directions.
3. Pour batter into a greased 13x18 baking sheet.
4. Bake in preheated oven for 15 minutes.
5. Mix together the pudding and milk.
6. Add the softened cream cheese to the pudding mixture and mix.
7. Fold in the cool whip.
8. Spread mixture on top of the cake.
9. Sprinkle the pineapple, coconut, and cherries on top.

Recipe courtesy of Sandy Newton

Chefnotes

To quickly toast coconut: place coconut on a paper plate, microwave for 15 to 30 seconds, then stir the coconut. Repeat until coconut is toasted.

Eclair Cake

2 small (3.4-ounce) packages instant french vanilla instant pudding

3½ cups milk

1 (8-ounce) container whipped topping

2½ (4.3-ounce) packages graham crackers

3 tablespoons margarine

2 teaspoons vanilla extract

2 teaspoons light corn syrup

6 tablespoons cocoa

2 tablespoons vegetable oil

3 tablespoons milk

1½ cups powdered sugar

1. In a large bowl mix together pudding and milk, and let sit several minutes.

2. Grease a 9x13 pan (butter or spray bottom and sides).

3. Line the bottom of the pan with whole pieces of graham crackers.

4. Spread half of the pudding on the graham crackers.

5. Add a second layer of graham crackers and then the remaining pudding.

6. Finally add a third layer of graham crackers.

7. Mix together margarine, vanilla, corn syrup, cocoa, oil, milk, and powdered sugar and spread on top of last layer of graham crackers.

8. Refrigerate for at least 2 hours, but preferably overnight.

Recipe courtesy of Sandy Newton

Chefnotes

☞ Can substitute 2 squares unsweetened chocolate for cocoa and oil.

Red Velvet Cake

Cake:

½ cup shortening

1½ cups white sugar

2 large eggs

½ cup red food coloring

2 tablespoons cocoa

1 teaspoon salt

1 teaspoon vanilla

1 cup buttermilk

2½ cups all-purpose flour, sifted

1 tablespoon vinegar

1 tablespoon baking

Frosting:

1 cup milk

5 tablespoons flour

½ cup (1 stick) butter

1 cup powdered sugar

1 teaspoon vanilla extract

1. Preheat oven to 350 ° F.

2. In a large bowl, cream together the shortening and sugar until fluffy.

3. Add the eggs, one at a time, to the sugar mixture, beating for one minute after adding each.

4. in a small bowl, mix together food coloring, cocoa, and salt, and then add to the main mixture.

5. Mix together vanilla and buttermilk. Then, alternate adding flour and buttermilk mixture to the batter.

6. Finally, mix together vinegar and baking soda, add to batter and beat just enough to combine.

7. Pour batter into a cake pan and bake at 350 ° F for 25 to 30 minutes.

8. For frosting, in a small saucepan, make a smooth paste with milk and flour. Cook till thick and then cool completely.

9. In a medium bowl, beat butter, powdered sugar, and vanilla till very creamy. Add cooled milk and flour mixture a little at a time to the powdered sugar mixture.

10. Frost cooled cake with frosting.

Recipe courtesy of Dave Newton

Cheesecake

1 (8-inch) graham cracker crust
1 (8-ounce) package cream cheese, softened
2 large eggs
½ cup white sugar
2 teaspoons vanilla extract
2 tablespoons lemon juice
8 ounces sour cream
2 tablespoons sugar
1 teaspoon vanilla
Fruit pie filling

1. Preheat oven to 350 ° F.

2. In a large bowl mix cream cheese until creamy.

3. Add eggs, sugar, vanilla and lemon juice and mix until creamy, smooth and runny.

4. Pour the mixture into the graham cracker crust.

5. Bake for 30 minutes at 350 ° F or until it shakes like solid gelatin.

6. In a medium bowl combine sour cream, sugar and vanilla, and mix well to form a sauce.

7. Spread Sauce on top of cheesecake and bake for 10 minutes more or until the sauce is also solid.

8. Chill for 4 hours or until cool.

9. Serve with fruit pie filling.

Recipe courtesy of Rebekah Emerson

St. Patrick's Day Cupcakes

makes 24 cupcakes   prep time: 30 minutes   cook time: 20 minutes

A few years ago, I made these for St. Patrick's day. They were super fun to make, looked nice, and tasted even better.

24 vanilla cupcakes, baked but not frosted

1 cup butter, softened

4½ cups powdered sugar

1 teaspoon vanilla extract

⅓ cup heavy cream

¼ teaspoon salt

4 drops green food coloring

12 AirHeads Xtremes Candy, Rainbow Berry flavor candies

3 cups mini marshmallows

24 Rolo candies

Gold sprinkles

1. **Frosting:** In a large bowl beat butter until creamy (with an electric mixer on medium high for about 2 minutes).

2. Add powdered sugar, vanilla, heavy cream, and salt and beat together until light and fluffy, about 3 minutes.

3. Add green food coloring until desired color is reached.

4. **Assemble:** Spread or pipe frosting on top of each cupcake.

5. Cut each Airheads candy in half and place on top of each cupcake to create an arch like a rainbow.

6. Place two mini marshmallows on each end of the rainbow for clouds.

7. To make the pot of gold, pipe a small amount of frosting onto the wide end of each Rollo, then press into gold sprinkles until all the frosting is covered.

8. Place on cupcake, gold side up.

Recipe courtesy of Libby Newton – adapted from Six Sisters' Stuff

Chefnotes

☙ I found perfect gold sprinkles for this at Walmart

Mona's Texas Sheet Cake
makes one 13x18 sheet cake

Oh Mona, I miss her. We all do. I miss going over to her house, eating one of her delicious meals, listening to the fight over cleaning up, and then ending with a game of cards. Ben and I are honored to have Mona's table in our home. The table where so many fun memories, and card games, were shared. I love to use it everyday adding our family memories to those with her.

A few times I asked her for recipes and that was always a crazy process. She was an artist cook who just put things together. Her love was not constrained by measurements. She gave me this recipe, but I had to ask a lot of clarifying questions to fill in the gaps.

We love it at our house. It is a frequent request for Ben's birthday cake. We have to be careful not to make it too often...because...well, try it and see for yourself.

Cake:
2 large eggs, beaten
½ cup milk
2 cups white sugar
2 cups all-purpose flour
½ teaspoon salt
1 teaspoon baking soda
1 cup (2 sticks) butter
4 tablespoons cocoa
1 cup water
1 teaspoon vanilla extract
Frosting:
½ cup (1 stick) butter
⅓ cup milk
4 tablespoons cocoa
1 pound powdered sugar
Nuts, optional

1. Preheat oven to 350 ° F.

2. In a large bowl combine eggs and milk. Mix in sugar, flour, salt and baking soda.

3. In a small saucepan melt butter and blend in cocoa and water.

4. Pour cocoa mixture into the large bowl, and mix to combine. Mix in vanilla. Batter will be runny. Worry not.

5. Grease or spray a 13x18 inch baking pan. Pour batter into the pan.

6. Bake in preheated oven until cake springs back in the middle. Let cake cool.

7. To make the frosting, in a small saucepan melt the butter, stir in the milk, cocoa, and powdered sugar. Frosting will be runny too. While frosting is still warm pour it it on and spread it over the mostly cooled cake. Let frosting cool and harden, then enjoy.

Recipe courtesy of Erin Newton – from Mona's own kitchen

Mona's paper says to mix the soda and the milk before adding it to the other things. I don't do that, but maybe it is magic...

If you happen to have gestational diabetes and just want a piece of this cake but only one with 15 grams of carbs...then cut a piece that is 1.5 inches by 2 inches. I know this because I have a kind and patient husband who calculated this for me when I was pregnant with Sam.

Sherry's Favorite Texas Chocolate Cake

Chocolate cake is my favorite treat. Put a slice in a bowl and pour some milk over the top, it may sound weird but I love to eat it this way, it reminds me of my dad who would eat it the same way. This cake recipe is the absolute best chocolate cake!

Cake:
2 cups all-purpose flour
½ teaspoon salt
2 cups white sugar
8 tablespoons (1 stick) butter
½ cup crisco
½ cup cocoa
1 cup water
½ cup buttermilk or sour milk
1 teaspoon baking soda
2 large eggs
1 teaspoon vanilla extract

Frosting:
1 stick of softened butter
2 cups powdered sugar

½ teaspoon vanilla
¾ teaspoon almond extract
3 to 4 tablespoons cocoa powder

1. **Cake:** Preheat oven to 400 ° F.
2. In a large bowl mix flour, salt and sugar.
3. In a saucepan melt butter and crisco, and mix in cocoa and water. Bring to a boil.
4. Pour chocolate mixture over flour and sugar. Blend until mixed.
5. Add remaining ingredients and beat until well blended.
6. Bake for 25 to 30 minutes.
7. **Frosting:** Add all frosting ingredients to bowl and mix until well blended.
8. Can add a bit of milk if consistency is too thick.
9. Frost cooled cake in a medium to thick layer.

Recipe courtesy of Sherry Poulsen

Chapter 14

Cookies

WHEN ERIN was in the hospital, sick with Covid-19, our kind friends brought us several meals, giving me one less thing to worry about while I attempted to juggle being both the mom and the dad for our four kids. Miraculously, for about five meals in a row, each wonderful dinner also included a plate of perfect homemade chocolate chip cookies. Wow, what a treat! It was as if we were presented with a chocolate chip cookie taste test. Each plate of cookies were different, some giant, some gooey, some with nuts, some without, but all were delicious. It's amazing how something as simple as a chocolate chip cookie can help convince you that everything's going to be okay. Hooray for cookies!

Ben Newton

White Chip Chocolate Cookies

1 cup (2 sticks) butter, softened
2 cups white sugar
2 large eggs
2 teaspoons vanilla extract
2 cups all-purpose flour
¾ cup cocoa
1 teaspoon baking soda
½ teaspoon salt
1⅔ cups white chocolate chips

1. Preheat oven to 350 ° F.
2. Beat butter and sugar in large bowl until creamy.
3. Add eggs and vanilla, beat until light and fluffy.
4. Stir in flour, cocoa, baking soda, and salt and beat into butter mixture.
5. Stir in white chocolate chips.
6. Drop rounded teaspoons onto a cookie sheet.
7. Bake for 8 to 9 minutes.

Recipe courtesy of Jen Burge

Favorite Chocolate Chip Cookies

makes 5 dozen cookies

This recipe came from a lady in my childhood neighborhood. It is my favorite and I don't stray from it because I know it is the best.

2 cups (4 sticks,1 pound) butter
1½ cups white sugar
2 cups brown sugar
3 large eggs
2 tablespoons vanilla extract
6 cups all-purpose flour
1½ teaspoons baking soda
1½ teaspoons salt
1 cup oatmeal
24 ounces chocolate chips

1. Preheat oven to 350 ° F.
2. Mix together butter, sugars, eggs, and vanilla.
3. Add in the remaining ingredients and mix.
4. Place rounded cookie dough mounds onto a baking sheet with a scoop.
5. Bake in preheated oven for 12 minutes.
6. Take cookies out of oven even if they appear not fully cooked.
7. Let cookies sit on cookie sheet for 5 minutes before transferring to a cooling rack.

Recipe courtesy of Jo Jacobs

Becky's Favorite Chocolate Chip Cookies

makes 4½ dozen cookies

2 ¼ cups all-purpose flour

1 teaspoon baking soda

1 teaspoon salt

1 cup (2 sticks) butter, softened

¾ cup granulated white sugar

¾ cup packed brown sugar

1 teaspoon vanilla extract

2 large eggs

1⅔ cups chocolate chips

1 cup chopped nuts

1. Preheat oven to 375° F.

2. In a small bowl, combine flour, baking soda and salt.

3. In a large mixing bowl, beat butter, granulated sugar, brown sugar and vanilla extract until creamy.

4. Add eggs, one at a time, beating well after each addition. Gradually beat in flour mixture. Stir in morsels and nuts.

5. Drop onto ungreased baking sheets by rounded tablespoon.

6. Bake for 9 to 11 minutes or until golden brown. Cool on baking sheets for 2 minutes; remove to wire racks to cool completely.

Recipe courtesy of Becky Robinson – from the back of a Nestle Toll House bag of chocolate chips

Food for Thought

Nuts are optional. If omitting, add 1 to 2 tablespoons of all-purpose flour

Sandy's Chocolate Chip Oatmeal Cookies

*T*his is my favorite cookie to make and to eat. It is one of those recipes that never fail. No matter how the dough looks, to moist or to dry they always turn out great.

1 cup white sugar

1 cup brown sugar

1 cup shortening

2 large eggs

1 teaspoon vanilla extract

2 cups all-purpose flour

1 teaspoon baking powder

1 teaspoon baking soda

½ teaspoon salt

2 cups old fashioned oats

1 cup coconut

1 cup chocolate chips

1. Preheat oven to 375 ° F
2. Cream together sugar, brown sugar, and shortening.
3. Add eggs and vanilla and mix.
4. Add the flour, baking powder, baking soda, and salt, and mix.
5. Slowly mix in the oatmeal, coconut and chocolate chips to form a very stiff cookie dough.
6. Drop by large spoonfuls onto ungreased cookie sheets.
7. Optionally, press down the cookies slightly with the bottom of a cup.
8. Bake in preheated oven for 8 to 10 minutes.

Recipe courtesy of Sandy Newton

Food for Thought

This recipe makes a very stiff cookie dough, which may require a hefty mixer.
An ice cream scoop often works well to spoon the cookies onto pans.

No-bake Cookies
makes 24 cookies

2 cups white sugar

3 tablespoons unsweetened cocoa powder

½ cup (1 stick) butter

½ cup milk

Pinch of salt

3 cups quick cooking oats

½ cup peanut butter or almond butter

1 teaspoon vanilla extract

1. In a saucepan bring sugar, cocoa, margarine, milk, and salt to a rapid boil for 1 minute.

2. Add oats, peanut butter, and vanilla; mix well.

3. Working quickly, drop by teaspoonfuls onto waxed paper, and let cool.

Recipe courtesy of Ben Newton – adapted from www.allrecipes.com/recipe/10745

Mrs. Field's Cookies

1½ cups white sugar

2 cups brown sugar

2 cups (4 sticks) butter

3 large eggs

2 teaspoons vanilla extract

4 cups chocolate chips

6 cups all-purpose flour

½ teaspoon salt

1½ teaspoons baking soda

2 cups raisins, nuts, or oatmeal (optional)

1. Preheat oven to 375 ° F.
2. In a large bowl, cream together sugar, brown sugar, and butter.
3. Mix in eggs and vanilla.
4. Add chocolate chips, flour, salt and soda and mix to combine.
5. Optionally, mix in raisins, nuts or oatmeal.
6. Bake in preheated oven for 8 to 10 minutes.

Recipe courtesy of Dave Newton

No-bake Chocolate Birds Nest Cookies

makes 12 servings   prep time: 10 minutes

1 (12-ounce) bag milk chocolate chips

1 (12-ounce) bag butterscotch chips

12 ounces chow mein noodles

1 cup M&Ms, Jellybean's, Chocolate eggs, or any other kind of "egg-shaped" candy

1. In a large microwave-safe bowl melt the chocolate chips and butterscotch chips in 60 second intervals stirring between each interval.

2. Repeat until chips are smoothly melted. Stir chow mein noodles in until all noodles are coated.

3. Lay out parchment or waxed paper and drop spoonfuls of chocolate coated noodles onto the paper.

4. Shape each mound into a bird's nest. Wash your hands well and then place a couple of egg shaped candies on top of each chocolate nest.

5. Let nests harden before serving.

Recipe courtesy of Libby Newton – from Six Sisters' Stuff

Chefnotes

Note, if you don't like butterscotch chips switch them out for white chocolate chips, peanut butter chips or a second bag of chocolate chips.

Grandma Barbara's Chocolate Macaroons

makes about 3½ dozen cookies

When Erin was young she could not eat wheat so making cookies for her was hard at times. She loved these macaroons though. These can be made with or without chocolate.

1 can sweetened condensed milk

4 squares unsweetened chocolate

¼ teaspoon salt

1 teaspoon vanilla extract

8 ounces shredded coconut

½ cup chopped nuts, optional

1. Preheat oven to 350 ° F. Generously grease two large baking sheets.

2. In the top of a double boiler combine milk, chocolate, and salt. Cook over hot water (not boiling) stirring frequently until mixture thickens, about 12 to 15 minutes.

3. Remove from heat. Mix in vanilla, then add coconut and nuts, if using. Mix well.

4. Drop by teaspoonfuls one inch apart on cookie sheets.

5. Bake in preheated oven for 10 minutes or just until cookies are set.

6. Remove at once with spatula to sheet of waxed paper or foil. Let cool.

Recipe courtesy of Deborah Robinson – from Grandma Barbara

Chocolate Crinkles

makes 72 cookies   prep time: 20 minutes   cook time: 12 minutes   total time: 5 hours

1 cup unsweetened cocoa powder

2 cups white sugar

½ cup vegetable oil

4 large eggs

2 teaspoons vanilla extract

2 cups all-purpose flour

2 teaspoons baking powder

½ teaspoon salt

½ cup confectioners' sugar

1. In a medium bowl, mix together cocoa, white sugar, and vegetable oil. Beat in eggs one at a time, then stir in the vanilla. Combine the flour, baking powder, and salt; stir into the cocoa mixture. Cover dough, and chill for at least 4 hours.

2. Preheat oven to 350 ° F. Line cookie sheets with parchment paper. Roll dough into one inch balls. Coat each ball in confectioners' sugar before placing onto prepared cookie sheets.

3. Bake in preheated oven for 10 to 12 minutes. Let stand on the cookie sheet for a minute before transferring to wire racks to cool.

Recipe courtesy of Sherry Poulsen – adapted from www.allrecipes.com/recipe/9861

Food for Thought

Consider using a number 50 size scoop to make dough balls.

Bryan's Swig Sugar Cookies

*B*ryan can grill, cook, and bake just about anything but one of his signature recipes is this sugar cookie recipe. While I was at work one Saturday, Bryan decided he wanted to make cookies with the boys. He found this recipe online and when I returned home I found these delicious cookies decorated pink and white with words like "I love Mom" on them, and of course there were blue and white frosted cookies with "BYU" on them.

Cookie Dough:

5½ cups all-purpose flour

½ teaspoon baking soda

½ teaspoon cream of tartar

1 teaspoon salt

1 cup butter

¾ cup vegetable oil

1½ cups white sugar, divided

¾ powdered sugar

2 tablespoons water

2 large eggs

Frosting:

½ cup butter, softened

¾ cup sour cream

1 teaspoon salt

5 cups powdered sugar

¼ cup milk

Food coloring, optional

1. **Cookies:**

2. Preheat oven to 350 ° F.

3. In a medium-sized mixing bowl combine flour, baking soda, cream of tartar, and salt; set aside.

4. In a large mixing bowl cream together butter, oil, 1 1/4 cups sugar, powdered sugar, and water. Mix in eggs.

5. Slowly add in the flour mixture until combined. Roll the dough into golf ball sized balls and place onto a cookie sheet.

6. To give the cookies their signature rough edge, dip the bottom of a glass into the reserved 1/4 cup sugar and press onto the cookie ball to flatten the cookie. You still want the cookie to be thick, so don't press them too thin.

7. Bake for 8 to 10 minutes. The cookies stay soft, so do not over bake.

8. **Frosting:** Cream together butter, sour cream, and salt. Add the powdered sugar and mix to combine. Then mix in milk until the desired consistency is reached. Optionally, mix in food coloring. Spread over cooled cookies.

Recipe courtesy of Bryan Burge

Great Grandma Newton's Famous Raisin Cookies

These cookies are the best! They were always a special treat around my house growing up. I would get a tinful on my birthday every year, even when I was on my mission in New Zealand. It took 6 weeks by boat to get there, and they were still delicious! Bet you can't eat just one!!

Cookies:

1 cup butter

2 cups white sugar

2 large eggs

4 tablespoons milk

½ teaspoon nutmeg

1 teaspoon vanilla extract

4½ cups all-purpose flour

1 teaspoon salt

4 teaspoons baking powder

Raisin filling:

½ cup sugar

1½ tablespoons cornstarch

1½ cups boiling water

3 cups raisins

1 tablespoon lemon juice

1. In a large bowl, cream together butter, 2 cups sugar and eggs.

2. In a small bowl, combine milk, nutmeg, and vanilla.

3. Sift together flour, salt and baking powder.

4. Alternate between adding the milk mixture then the flour mixture to the butter mixture, until well combined.

5. Chill dough for 1 hour.

6. For the raisin filling, in a medium saucepan, mix together 1/2 cup sugar and cornstarch.

7. Pour 1 1/2 cups boiling water over the sugar mixture and stir.

8. Add raisins and bring to a boil while stirring, allowing the mixture to thicken and all the liquid to evaporate. Remove from heat.

9. Stir in lemon juice.

10. Preheat oven to 375 ° F.

11. To assemble cookies, remove chilled dough from the refrigerator, and roll out half of the dough to 1/8 to 3/16 inch thickness.

12. Using a 3" round or scalloped cookie cutter, cut out cookie bottoms and place on a baking sheet.

13. Place a spoonful of the raisin mixture on each cookie bottom.

14. Roll out the remainder of the dough to the same thickness, and cut out cookie tops with same cookie cutter.

15. Using your finger or a pastry brush; run a bit of milk around the edge of cookie bottom (to help seal the top and bottom dough together).

16. Place a cookie top on each cookie bottom pressing the edges together to seal.

17. Use a fork to prick holes in the top of each cookie.

18. Bake in preheated oven for 10 to 12 minutes.

19. Hide the cookies where only you can find them! They are so.....good!

Recipe courtesy of Dave Newton

Bryan's Peanut Butter Cookies

makes 24 cookies   prep time: 20 minutes   cook time: 18 minutes

1⅓ cup (188g) all-purpose flour
¾ teaspoon baking soda
½ teaspoon baking powder
¼ teaspoon salt
½ cup (113g) unsalted butter, softened
½ cup (105g) granulated white sugar
½ cup (110g) packed light brown sugar
¾ cup (185g) creamy peanut butter
1 large egg
1½ teaspoons vanilla extract

1. Preheat oven to 350° F. Line two 18 by 13-inch baking sheets with silicone baking liners or parchment paper.

2. In a medium mixing bowl whisk together flour (be sure to level when measuring), baking soda, baking powder, and salt. Set aside.

3. In the bowl of an electric stand mixer fitted with the paddle attachment cream together butter, granulated sugar, and brown sugar until combined.

4. Mix in peanut butter then blend in egg and vanilla. With mixer set on low speed slowly add in flour mixture and mix just until combined.

5. Scoop dough out and shape into balls (30 grams each or nearly 2 tablespoons) then place on baking sheets spacing them 2-inches apart.

6. Using a long pronged fork flatten cookies slightly then turn fork going opposite direction and flatten just slightly again (it should create a criss-cross pattern).

7. Bake cookies in preheated oven, one sheet at a time, for about 9 minutes (cookies will appear pale and slightly underbaked, they'll continue to cook slightly as they cool).

8. Let cool on baking sheet 5 minutes then transfer to a wire rack to cool completely. Store cookies and an airtight container.

Recipe courtesy of Bryan Burge – from www.cookingclassy.com/classic-peanut-butter-cookies

Sherry's Snickerdoodle Cookies

1 cup shortening
1½ cups white sugar
2 large eggs
2¾ cups all-purpose flour
2 teaspoons cream of tartar
1 teaspoon vanilla extract
1 teaspoon baking soda
½ teaspoon salt

1. Preheat oven to 400° F.

2. In a large bowl cream shortening and sugar.

3. Mix in eggs and vanilla, and then remaining ingredients.

4. Shape dough into 1-inch balls and roll each in equal parts of cinnamon and sugar, and place on a baking sheet.

5. Flatten with the bottom of a glass.

6. Bake in preheated oven for 10 minutes.

Recipe courtesy of Sherry Poulsen

Emily Ann Robinson's Snickerdoodles

1 cup shortening
1½ cups white sugar
2 large eggs
2¾ cups sifted all-purpose flour
2 teaspoons cream of tartar
1 teaspoon baking soda
½ teaspoon salt
2 tablespoons sugar

2 teaspoons cinnamon.

1. Preheat oven to 400 ° F.

2. Cream shortening and sugar together. Mix in eggs. Add flour, cream of tartar, baking soda and salt, and mix. Form dough into balls about the size of a walnut and roll in sugar and cinnamon. Place on a baking sheet then bake for 8 to 10 minutes in preheated oven.

Recipe courtesy of Becky Robinson – from Emily Ann Robinson

Sugar and Spice Cookies

makes 24 cookies   prep time: 10 minutes   cook time: 13 minutes

We were trying to have an authentic Nauvoo Christmas in the American Fork 1st ward. Apparently, Emma Smith threw a Christmas party one year and they had gingerbread cookies for dessert. The lady in charge of the party wanted everything to be super true to life but many of us thought that gingerbread cookies alone wouldn't appeal to many people. Sis. Jackie Nelson makes these sugar and spice cookies every Christmas and thought they would be a good compromise. I have never liked gingerbread or anything with molasses in it but these are amazing!

¾ cup butter
1 cup white sugar
1 large egg
¼ cup molasses
2 cups all-purpose flour
1 teaspoon cinnamon
2 teaspoons baking soda
¾ teaspoon cloves
¼ teaspoon salt
¾ teaspoon ginger

1. Preheat oven to 325 ° F.

2. Combine the butter, sugar, egg, and molasses in a mixing bowl and mix.

3. Combine the other dry ingredients separately and sift them.

4. Combine the dry ingredients with the mixed ingredients. Roll into balls and roll into sugar. We use both demerara sugar and regular white sugar for this.

5. Cook at 325 ° F for 13 minutes.

Recipe courtesy of Rose Frank – from Jackie Nelson of the American Fork 1st ward

Gingerbread Persons

makes approximately 2 dozen cookies or a handful of gingerbread persons

When Emma was in Joy School, I started making these gingerbread persons. It really is a gingery joy!

4½ cups all-purpose flour

4 teaspoons ground ginger

2 teaspoons baking soda

1½ teaspoons ground cinnamon

1 teaspoon ground cloves

¼ teaspoon salt

1½ cups shortening (or half shortening and half butter)

2 cups white sugar

2 large eggs

½ cup molasses

Chocolate chips, for decorating, optional

1. In a medium bowl stir together flour, ginger, baking soda, cinnamon, cloves, and salt, then set aside. In a large mixing bowl beat shortening with an electric mixer, then add the sugar and cream together. Beat in eggs and molasses until combined. Finally, beat in as much flour as you can, then stir in any remaining flour.

2. Preheat oven to 350° F.

3. If you are making gingerbread men or women, now the fun begins. Make a personal cooking sheet for each gingerbeing out of foil. Make one head-sized ball of dough (about 1 1/2 inch in diameter), one body-sized ball of dough (about 2 inch in diameter), and four arm and leg-sized balls of dough (about 1 inch in diameter) for each gingerbeing. Then squish or roll the dough balls into the head shape, body shape, and arm and leg shapes, and join together to make a person. If desired, use large and small chocolate chips for eyes, mouth, nose, and front buttons. Bake in preheated oven for about 10 minutes or until the bottom is browned and the top is puffy. Be careful when you open the oven, do not let the gingerperson jump out!

4. Otherwise, if you are not making gingerbread persons at this time...worry not, they are still fun to eat as gingerbread cookies. Shape dough into two inch balls using a 1/4 cup measuring cup or scoop. Roll balls in some additional coarse or fine white sugar. Place dough balls two inches apart on an ungreased cookie sheet.

5. Bake in preheated oven for 11 to 13 minutes or until edges are lightly browned and the tops are puffy. Be careful not to overbake.

Recipe courtesy of Erin Newton – adapted from Better Homes and Gardens Cookbook

Food for Thought

In my experience it is best to read "The Gingerbread Man" when making this recipe with kids, either ahead of time, while the cookies are baking, or while eating them!

Chefnotes

☞ Best made with the help of children. Also, don't forget the milk in the eating phase.

Lion House Sugar Cookies

1 1⁄2 cups white sugar

2⁄3 cup butter

2 large eggs, beaten

2 tablespoons milk

1 teaspoon vanilla extract

3 1⁄4 cups all-purpose flour

2 1⁄2 teaspoons baking powder

1⁄2 teaspoon salt

1. Cream butter and sugar.
2. Mix in eggs, milk and vanilla.
3. Sift flour, baking powder, and salt together. Add to creamed mixture. Combine thoroughly.
4. With hands shape dough into a ball.
5. Wrap with plastic wrap and refrigerate 2 to 3 hours or overnight.
6. Preheat oven to 400 ° F.
7. Grease cookie sheets lightly.
8. On lightly floured board or counter, roll 1/2 to 1/3 of dough at a time, keeping rest in fridge.
9. For soft cookies, roll 1/8 to 1/4 inch thick.
10. Cut with floured cookie cutter. Place 1/2 inch apart on cookie sheet.
11. Bake in preheated oven for 8 minutes or until a very light brown.

Recipe courtesy of Ben Newton – from the Lion House

Great Grandma Marie Newton's Shortbread

*E*very Christmas Grandma would make shortbread for all her children and grandchildren. That was a lot of butter encased in a lot of shortbread, for a lot of grandchildren! I loved to eat the large shortbread cookies piece by piece during the Christmas break. I got the recipe from my Dad after he helped Grandma make shortbread one Christmas.

2 cups (4 sticks) butter

2 cups white sugar

1 large egg

1 teaspoon vanilla extract

4 to 5 cups all-purpose flour

1. In a large bowl cream together the butter, sugar, egg, and vanilla until well combined. Slowly stir in the flour.

2. Optionally, refrigerate for 1 hour.

3. Preheat oven to 350°F.

4. Roll out dough to a 1/4 inch thickness, cut into desired shapes, and transfer to baking sheets.

5. Bake in preheated oven for 15 to 20 minutes.

Recipe courtesy of Ben Newton

Chefnotes

Grandma's cookies were always large, about 4 to 6 inches across, with huge cookies for the adults and slightly smaller, but still plenty big, cookies for the children. Each cookie had indentations around the edge (presumably from pressing fingers into the dough around the edge prior to cooking).

Chapter 15

Candies

Y EARS AGO I was sitting on the couch watching a Christmas show. I remember that I knew my dad was making something with caramel, but I wasn't sure what. While he was cooking, I kept checking on him and looking to see what he was making. After a while, I came back found that he was making carmel corn! It was wonderful and looked delicious. He gave me a few pieces, then we took it to our friends and neighbors. I loved seeing their happy faces when we gave them the treat.

Emmalyn Newton - age 11

Taffy

*E*very once in a while, perhaps in our less sane moments, we make taffy with our kids. We make the candy, and then with buttered hands, allow everyone to take turns pulling it. I don't know that we've every made perfect taffy, but we've certainly made wonderful memories.

2 ½ cups white sugar

3 tablespoons cornstarch

1 cup corn syrup

1 ⅓ cups water

2 tablespoons butter

½ teaspoon salt

1 (0.13 ounce) package unsweetened, powdered drink mix.

1. Butter 2 large baking sheets, and set them aside.

2. In a medium saucepan, stir together the sugar and cornstarch. Add the corn syrup, water, butter and salt, and stir to blend. Bring to a boil over medium heat, and cook until the mixture reads 250 ° F on a candy thermometer. Remove from heat, and immediately stir in the powdered drink mix. This will add color and flavoring to the candy. Quickly pour out onto the prepared baking sheets, and let stand until cool enough to handle.

3. Grab a few helpers, and butter everyone's hands. Pull the taffy by stretching it and then folding it back on itself over and over again until it lightens in color, and becomes firm. Roll into several long ropes about an inch thick, and then cut into 1-inch pieces with scissors. Wrap each candy in a small square of waxed paper or plastic wrap.

Recipe courtesy of Ben Newton – from www.allrecipes.com/recipe/42673

Food for Thought

Make sure you have a working candy thermometer when you make this, otherwise you'll likely end up with something other than taffy.

Homemade Peppermint Patties

makes 28 patties   total time: 2 hours

Recently, I tried this recipe because I love York peppermint patties. It is really good. However, the first time I made it I thought it would be a great idea to use a wire rack. A few second after I set each patty on the rack, they started to melt everywhere and made a huge mess! That is what we call a messipe.

¾ cup sweetened condensed milk

1½ teaspoons peppermint extract

4 cups powdered sugar

3 cups semi-sweet chocolate chips

2 teaspoons shortening

1. Line a baking sheet with parchment or wax paper.
2. In a large mixing bowl combine sweetened condensed milk and peppermint extract.
3. With an electric mixer beat in the powdered sugar a little at a time until a stiff dough starts to form and the dough is no longer sticky.
4. Form dough into 1-inch balls then place on prepared baking sheet flatten each ball with the bottom of a cup or your palm to form patties.
5. Let patties dry at room temperature for 2 hours flipping over after an hour to set evenly on both sides
6. After 2 hours place the Pan in the freezer for 30 minutes.
7. Meanwhile, melt chocolate and shortening in a saucepan over low heat stirring often until smooth.
8. Remove chocolate from heat and let cool for a few minutes. Remove patties from freezer and dip them into chocolate one at a time by resting them on the tines of a fork and lowering the fork into the chocolate until all sides are covered, then raising the fork and letting the excess chocolate drip off.
9. Place dipped patties back on the parchment paper or wax paper and let cool until chocolate is set.

Recipe courtesy of Libby Newton – from Six Sisters' Stuff

Chefnotes

🎩 I used a double boiler for the chocolate. We don't have a real one so I used a glass bowl over a pan of boiling water.

Grandma Barbara's Surprise Popcorn Balls

These are one of Brion's favorite treats at Christmas. Years ago, after some importuning I finally made them for him and they have been a family favorite ever since. One caution: I suggest you buy the ingredients just before you are ready to make them. If not, it can get pricey to replace the cashews that were eaten as a snack. Also, the red and green spiced gumdrops are sometimes hard to find. You may also find it wise to cut this recipe down. It makes a prodigious amount of popcorn balls, which is okay if your family is large or you are giving some as gifts. If not, and you make the full recipe, you may gain some weight and you'll be picking hulls out of your mouth for days.

4 quarts (roughly 16 cups) popped popcorn
2 cups roasted and salted cashews
1½ cups spiced red and green gumdrops
3 cups mini marshmallows
1 cup (2 sticks) butter
1½ cups white sugar
½ cup light Karo syrup
1 teaspoon vanilla extract

1. Pop the popcorn. (Can use the microwave so as to not have to use oil to pop it. You will have to do several batches till you have enough.)
2. Place the popped popcorn in a very large bowl, leaving out any hulls and unpopped kernels. This is a little tedious, but it makes a much nicer product.
3. Mix in the cashews, gumdrops, and marshmallow to the popcorn.
4. In a large saucepan over medium heat, melt the butter. As it begins to melt add the sugar, and Karo syrup. Bring to a rolling boil over medium high heat (at this point the mixture won't reduce much when you stir it).
5. Boil for 3 minutes and remove from heat.
6. Add vanilla while stirring. Pour the hot syrup mixture over the popcorn, cashews, gumdrops and marshmallows and stir with a large wooden spoon till everything is coated and it is cool enough to handle.
7. Have an extra stick of butter ready to grease your hands before forming whatever size balls you want. The butter keeps the popcorn from sticking to your hands. The popcorn will cool quickly and become firm, but handle with care as you begin. Candy burns hurt a lot!

Recipe courtesy of Deborah Robinson – from Grandma Barbara

Food for Thought

Have a bowl ready large enough to mix all the ingredients together after syrup is finished and ready to pour. Make it large! Mixing this together can also be messy and painful if you slop the hot mixture onto your skin

You will notice that as the candy coating is boiling it will at first bubble up, but when it reaches that rolling boil stage the bubbles become smaller and pull down into the mixture.

I try to use whole cashews.

You can use any color of spiced gumdrops if you cannot find red and green. I don't generally like spiced gumdrops, but they are quite good in this mixture.

Sandy's Oven Caramel Corn

2 cups brown sugar

1 cup (2 sticks) butter

½ to 1 teaspoon salt

½ cup white corn syrup

1 teaspoon butter flavoring, optional

½ teaspoon vanilla extract

½ teaspoon baking soda

24 to 32 cups (6 to 8 quarts) popped popcorn (about ¾ cup popping corn)

1. Preheat oven to 225 ° F.

2. In a saucepan combine brown sugar, butter or margarine, salt, corn syrup, and butter flavoring, if using, and boil for 5 minutes.

3. Remove from heat and stir in vanilla and baking soda. It will foam while stirring.

4. Working quickly and carefully, pour mixture over the popcorn, and stir until well coated.

5. Spread half of the coated popcorn onto each of two 13x18 baking sheets.

6. Cook in preheated oven for 1 hour, stirring every 15 minutes.

7. Remove popcorn from pans and let cool.

Recipe courtesy of Sandy Newton and Becky Robinson

Chefnotes

☞ Becky Robinson also makes this wonderful treat. She uses 1/2 to 1 teaspoon salt, and leaves out the butter flavoring, whereas Sandy uses 1 teaspoon salt and the butter flavoring. Becky also suggests boiling the mixture without stirring and cooking at a lower temperature of 200 degrees F.

Chapter 16

Other Desserts

THE WORD DESSERT will make just about anyone smile. I love the way that desserts smell, the way they make people happy, the way they make a celebration special, and the way they can heal an aching heart or body. However, the thing I love most about dessert is the way that it brings people together. There is something almost magical about the whole thing. We all sit down and eat dinner together and then all get up from the table and do our own different things. But when it's time for dessert, we all come back together, with excited giggles and smiles, and eat a sweet treat together. I love it!

Growing up, I was always drawn to making desserts. I don't have the best memory, but I can remember, as a small child, standing on the step stool next to my mother as we made cookies together; scooping the flour and sugar out of the drawers in the island cabinets and pouring in the chocolate chips. It still brings a smile to my face. I'm pretty sure I inherited my "sweet tooth" from my mom and I loved baking with her and learning from her.

The dessert traditions have carried over to my family. My boys love to make sweet treats with me and I love standing next to them as we create those memories. Desserts are the best, and in my house a dessert is a completely acceptable breakfast!!!

Jen Burge

Pumpkin Chocolate Chip Bread

*W*henever I make this recipe I ALWAYS double it, because I want to eat one whole loaf by myself! (I don't, I just want to.)

½ cup butter

1 cup white sugar

2 large eggs

1¾ cups all-purpose flour

½ teaspoon nutmeg

⅓ teaspoon ginger

1 teaspoon cinnamon

¼ teaspoon cloves

1 teaspoon baking soda

½ teaspoon salt

¾ cup pumpkin purée

¾ cup chocolate chips

1. Preheat oven to 350 ° F.

2. Cream butter, sugar, and eggs together.

3. Add remaining ingredients and mix until fully incorporated.

4. Place in sugar coated loaf pan sprinkle sugar on the top of each loaf and bake at 350 ° F for 40 to 45 minutes.

Recipe courtesy of Rose Frank

Jenny's Caramel Brownies

1 (15.25-ounce) package German chocolate cake mix

⅔ cup evaporated milk

¾ cup margarine

1 (14-ounce) package of caramels

1 (6-ounce) package of milk chocolate chips

1. Grease a 9 x 13 baking dish and preheat oven to 350 ° F.

2. Mix cake mix, half (1/3 cup) evaporated milk, and margarine until moist.

3. Spread half of the batter on the bottom of the greased baking dish. Bake for 6 minutes.

4. Meanwhile, melt caramels and 1/3 cup of evaporated milk in the top of a double boiler or in the microwave for 2 minutes or until melted.

5. Remove pan from oven and pour caramel mixture over cooked batter. Sprinkle chocolate chips over caramel mixture, then blob remaining batter on top.

6. Bake for an additional 18 to 20 minutes.

Recipe courtesy of Stacy Schultz – from Jenny Burge

Grandma Nancy's Mint Fudge Brownies

*T*his is one of my personal favorites that I ask my Grandma Nancy to make any chance I get!

Brownies:

6 large eggs

3 cups sugar

5 squares unsweetened chocolate

½ cup (1 stick) butter

1 cup (2 sticks) margarine

3 teaspoons pure peppermint extract

2¼ cups all-purpose flour

Frosting:

10 tablespoons butter, melted

5 cups powdered sugar

5 to 7 teaspoons milk

5 teaspoons pure peppermint extract

Drizzle:

6 tablespoons butter, softened

3 squares unsweetened chocolate

1. **Brownies:** Preheat oven to 350° F.

2. In a large bowl, beat together eggs and sugar until well beaten, set aside.

3. In a small saucepan melt 5 squares unsweetened chocolate. When almost melted add 1 stick butter and 2 sticks margarine. Allow to melt, and mix together. Add 3 teaspoons pure peppermint extract.

4. Pour chocolate mixture into egg and sugar mixture, and mix to combine, then mix in flour.

5. Grease and flour a jelly roll pan (15.5x10.5-inch) and pour brownie batter into the pan.

6. Bake in preheated oven for 30 minutes.

7. Take out and cool in freezer for 5 to 10 minutes.

8. **Frosting:** In a large bowl cream together softened butter, powdered sugar, milk, and 5 teaspoons pure peppermint extract.

9. Frost brownies then return to freezer for 10 minutes.

10. **Drizzle Topping:** Mix together 6 tablespoons melted butter and 3 squares unsweetened chocolate.

11. Drizzle over on top of the frosted brownies.

12. Return once again to the freezer for 10 to 15 minutes.

13. Cut and keep refrigerated until served.

Recipe courtesy of Jo Jacobs

Easy Dutch Oven Peach Cobbler

*W*henever we go camping my kids beg me to make this easy dutch oven dessert.

25 charcoal briquettes

2 (15-ounce) cans sliced peaches in syrup

1 (15 to 16-ounce) package of cake mix (white, yellow, or spiced)

1 stick butter

Ground cinnamon, optional

1. Light 25 briquettes. In about 15 minutes, when edges of the coals turn white, the charcoal will be ready to use.

2. Meanwhile, pour peaches into the dutch oven and spread the dry cake mix evenly over them.

3. Optionally, sprinkle cinnamon over peaches and cake mix, to taste.

4. Cut butter into slices and place at various locations on top of the cake mix. Place lid on top of oven.

5. Place dutch oven over 15 hot briquettes. Add remaining 10 briquettes to the top of the dutch oven.

6. After 30 minutes, remove a few coals from the bottom of the dutch oven and place them on top of the dutch oven (to complete the browning process on the top of the cobbler). Bake for about 15 more minutes or until browned on top. Spoon out cobbler and serve in bowls.

Recipe courtesy of Ben Newton – adapted from www.delish.com

Sherry's Derby Pie

A beautiful, rich, chocolate pecan pie that Sherry would often make for Thanksgiving.

3 large eggs

⅔ cup white sugar

½ teaspoon salt

⅓ cup melted butter

1 cup light corn syrup

1 pie crust

¾ cup chopped pecans

¾ cup chocolate chips

1. Preheat oven to 375 ° F.

2. Place eggs, sugar, salt, melted butter, and corn syrup in a blender and blend until well combined.

3. Pour the mixture into the pie crust.

4. Sprinkle the pecans and chocolate chips over the mixture and stir them into the pie.

5. Bake for 40 to 50 minutes.

Recipe courtesy of Sherry Poulsen

Banana Cream Pie

Crust:

1 ¼ cup graham-cracker crumbs, about 10 or 11 whole crackers

1 teaspoon white sugar

4 tablespoons butter, melted

Pastry cream:

1 ⅔ cups milk

¼ cup plus 3 tablespoons sugar

½ tablespoon vanilla

3 tablespoons cornstarch

1 large egg

2 large egg yolks

1 ½ tablespoons butter

Assembly:

1 ½ cups heavy cream

¼ cup sour cream

3 ½ medium bananas, sliced into⅜-inch-thick rounds

1. **Crust:** Preheat oven to 325 ° F.

2. In a bowl, combine the crumbs and sugar. Add the butter and mix, first with a fork, then with your fingers, until the crumbs are moistened. Pour the mixture into a 9-inch pie pan, using a flat-bottomed cup to press the crumbs evenly. The edges of the shell will be crumbly. Bake until lightly browned, 9 or 10 minutes. Cool completely.

3. **Pastry cream:** In a medium saucepan over medium heat, combine the milk, 1/4 cup sugar and the vanilla and bring to a simmer. In a small bowl mix 3 tablespoons sugar and the cornstarch. In a large bowl, whisk together the egg and yolks.

4. When the milk comes to a simmer, discard the vanilla bean. Add the cornstarch mixture to the eggs and whisk until well combined.

5. While whisking the egg mixture, slowly pour in about 1/4 of the milk. Transfer this mixture into the saucepan, set over low heat and simmer, whisking constantly, until it reaches the consistency of thick pudding. (Be careful not to curdle the eggs.) Remove from the heat and stir in the butter until incorporated. Pour into a shallow bowl, place plastic wrap directly on the surface and chill.

6. **Assembly:** Using an electric mixer or a whisk, whip the heavy cream and sour cream into peaks. Transfer the pastry cream to a large bowl and whisk until smooth. Fold in 1/2 cup of the whipped cream. Line the bottom of the cooled pie shell with a layer of bananas. Optionally mash the remaining bananas. Fold the remaining bananas into the pastry cream, then spoon it evenly into the shell. Mound the remaining whipped cream on top, swirling it decoratively. Chill and serve within 24 hours.

Recipe courtesy of Emma Newton – from cooking.nytimes.com/recipes/11172-banana-cream-pie

Sweet Potato Pie
makes 6 to 8 servings

*L*iving in North Carolina we were exposed to "southern cookin'" of all types. From shrimp and grits to fried green tomatoes, and from Carolina barbecue to chicken and waffles, we were immersed in southern food. So, it seemed only natural that I should learn to make sweet potato pie. This has been one of my favorite pies ever since.

Filling:
2 pounds sweet potatoes, for 1½ cups puree
¼ cup (½ stick) butter
Pinch salt
3 eggs
½ cup sugar
1 cup heavy cream
1 tablespoon grated orange zest
1 teaspoon ground cinnamon
½ teaspoon ground nutmeg

Pastry:
1¼ cups all-purpose flour
1 tablespoon white sugar
Pinch salt
½ cup (1 stick) butter, cold and cut into small chunks
2 tablespoons ice water, plus more if needed
1 large egg white, lightly beaten

Topping:
½ cup pecans
1 (8-ounce) package frozen cranberries
2 to 3 ounces of cookies, such as amaretto cookies or rum-flavored cookies.

1. **Crust:** Preheat the oven to 375 ° F.
2. Prick the sweet potatoes with a fork and bake them until they are soft, about 1 hour. Remove from the oven and set aside until they are cool enough to handle.
3. **While the potatoes are cooking, make the pastry:** combine the flour, sugar, and salt in a large mixing bowl. Add the butter and mix with a pastry blender or your hands until the mixture resembles coarse crumbs. Pour in the ice water and work it in to bind the dough until it holds together without being too wet or sticky. Squeeze a small amount together, if it is crumbly, add more ice water, 1 teaspoon at a time. Form the dough into a ball, wrap it in plastic wrap, and refrigerate it for at least 30 minutes.
4. Sprinkle the counter and a rolling pin lightly with flour. Roll the dough out into a 10-inch circle. Carefully roll the dough up onto the pin and lay it inside a 9-inch pie pan. (This recipe won't fit a larger pie dish without modification.) Press the dough firmly into the bottom and sides so it fits tightly. Trim the excess dough around the rim and pinch the edges to form a border. Place a piece of parchment paper over the crust and fill with uncooked beans or pie weights. Bake the pie crust at 375 ° F until it sets, about 20 minutes. Remove the parchment and beans. Brush the bottom with the beaten egg white and set aside.
5. **While the crust is cooking make the filling:** When cool enough to handle, peel the sweet potatoes and puree the pulp in a food processor with 1/2 stick butter and a pinch of salt. Measure 1 1/2 cups puree into a bowl. In another bowl beat the eggs and sugar until the sugar has dissolved. Add the eggs to the sweet potato puree and whisk well. Add the cream, orange zest, cinnamon, and nutmeg and stir well to combine. Pour the mixture into the pie shell. Place the pie pan on a sturdy cookie sheet to catch any spills. Lower the oven temperature to 325 ° F and bake until the pie is set but still jiggles slightly, about 40 minutes. Remove

from the oven and allow it to cool.

6. **Topping:** Meanwhile, put the pecans on a baking sheet and bake them with the pie for about 10 minutes to toast them. Remove them from the oven and let them cool. Thaw the cranberries in a strainer set over a bowl to catch the liquid. Put the cookies, pecans, and cranberries into a food processor and pulse them a few times until they are coarsely chopped. Sprinkle the topping evenly over the cooled pie and serve immediately.

Recipe courtesy of Ben Newton – from www.foodnetwork.com/recipes/tyler-florence

Chocolate Strawberry pie

makes 8 slices

*O*nce I tried to make a chocolate tart for a Halloween Party using chocolate ganache, and it turned out far too thick and rich. But that didn't stop me from eating it a little bit at a time...I was sitting on my kitchen floor eating chocolate out of the pie pan with a spoon one morning when my roommate Krysta came into the kitchen and said "Ooh! Chocolate!" She got a spoon and sat on the floor to eat out of the pie pan with me, and we ate chocolate until she realized she was late for work, so I drove here there much too fast. That was the day we became best friends. I kept trying to fix the recipe, and a year and a half later, I made this pie for Krysta's birthday and it was a triumph!

¾ cup heavy whipping cream

1½ cups semisweet chocolate (I use good chocolate chips, but baking chocolate technically is higher quality with a less waxy texture, so if you're really serious, chop up a baking bar instead.)

1 pie crust (whatever you want, I'm not the expert here)

1 pound strawberries

1. Put the chocolate chips in some container that is deep enough to hold both the chocolate and the cream. (I usually put it straight into the metal mixing bowl of my KitchenAid, already attached. If you have to move it or touch it, use plastic or glass.)

2. Heat the cream in a small saucepan on the stove.

3. The cream needs to be just about to boil, but not actually boiling. If it boils, start over cause the texture will be toast. Once the cream just starts to bubble and shake, pour it over the chocolate. Make sure all the chocolate is level and covered.

4. Leave the chocolate and cream alone without stirring for 5 to 7 minutes. Don't touch it.

5. To combine them, I recommend using a stand mixer, but a hand mixer will work as well. Beat on low speed until the chocolate and cream are totally combined. It will start out looking like chocolate milk and you might think it will never actually work, but it will. Once the chocolate is smooth and glossy, scrape down the sides of the bowl and stir again to make sure all the cream is combined.

6. Now you've got ganache, and it is beautiful. However, the trick to making a fantastic pie is to whip it. (It doesn't look like enough chocolate to fill a pie, but whipping also doubles the volume.)

7. This will take a loooong time if you just use a whisk- you need something electric for this. Whip on medium-high speed for a few minutes until the chocolate changes color. Once it lightens up and looks more like milk chocolate, stop the mixer and check the texture. It should be airy and lighter, but not super stiff. It's somewhere between a whipped cream and a mousse.

8. Don't use the highest speed for too long or overmix or you will end up with chocolate butter. (Which is not the worst fate in the world, but doesn't make great pie. Dip fruit in it and move on if this happens;)

9. Wash your strawberries.

10. Choose the best, biggest, most uniform four or five strawberries to save for the top, and dice the rest into small pieces.

11. Get your already prepared and cooled pie crust, and pour in some of the chocolate (about a cup, enough to coat the bottom of the pie crust.)

12. Add your diced strawberries onto this layer of chocolate, then cover with the rest of the chocolate

and smooth out.

13. Cut your remaining strawberries in half and place in a circle around the edge of the pie, with one uncut strawberry stuck in the middle.

14. Chill for at least half an hour, until the pie is more set but not too stiff.

15. You'll want to eat it within a day or two, because the strawberries will sweat their own juice and leak onto the chocolate. It'll get sticky and less attractive if you leave it for too long.

Recipe courtesy of Amy Koeven – inspired by LaChelle Hansen

Food for Thought

When I made the pie for Krysta's birthday, mom helped me make the pie crust. I have tried since then to make good pie crust without much success. Pie crust is just not in my soul. So....I have nothing worthwhile to tell you about the crust here. Do whatever. The chocolate is the point anyway.

This works just as well with raspberries in pie form. (Maybe better, because the raspberries don't leach juice the way strawberries do.)

I sometimes add an extract into the ganache for extra flavor. Coconut or lemon works really well with raspberries. I've done a whole chocolate orange theme too. Do whatever your heart desires. When adding extract into the ganache, do it just as soon as you start to whip, and add about 1/8 of a teaspoon, the smallest amount you can add and still be adding something. Half a capful is too much!

Chefnotes

I originally started making chocolate ganache using a recipe from sugarduchess.com (which is no longer there, sorry). LaChelle Hansen, little sister of Erin's best friend Sherrie Boren, is the original architect and inspiration.

Peach Pie

makes 6 servings   prep time: 15 minutes   cook time: 50 minutes   total time: 1 hour and 5 minutes

*P*ies are beautiful creations! This peach pie is no exception. Weaving a lattice top onto a peach or apple pie can be a great achievement for a young chef.

2 store bought or homemade pie crusts

32 ounces of canned peaches, drained

1 cup granulated white sugar

1 tablespoon vanilla extract

1 tablespoon lemon juice

½ teaspoon ground cinnamon

¼ teaspoon ground nutmeg

½ cup all-purpose flour

1½ teaspoons butter, melted

1 large egg, beaten

1. Preheat oven to 350 ° F.
2. Make homemade crust and place in a 9 inch pie pan, or place store bought crust in pie and and set aside.
3. In a large mixing bowl mix the peaches, sugar, vanilla, lemon juice, cinnamon, and nutmeg. Stir until well combined.
4. Sprinkle in the flour, and fold into the ingredients until everything is well incorporated.
5. Fold in the butter.
6. Pour the peach mixture into the crust.
7. Top with the remaining crust. You can leave the crust whole or weave a lattice top.
8. Brush the crust with the beaten egg.
9. Bake in the preheated oven for 50 to 55 minutes.
10. Serve with vanilla ice cream.

Recipe courtesy of Ben Newton – adapted from iheartrecipes.com/grandmas-peach-pie/

Sweet Pie Crusts

makes two 9-inch single crust pies or one 9-inch double-crust pie

Recently we bought a food processor, which has been awesome for many things, including making pie crusts. This recipe came with the food processor, and it makes wonderfully sweet and flaky pie crusts with a hint of lemon and vanilla.

2 cups unbleached, all-purpose flour

2 tablespoons white sugar

½ teaspoon kosher salt

12 tablespoons (1½ sticks, ¾ cup) butter

2 large egg yolks

1 tablespoon ice water

¼ teaspoon lemon zest (optional)

½ teaspoon pure vanilla extract

1. Insert the chopping blade in a food processor. Add the flour, sugar and salt and process for 10 seconds to sift.

2. Add the butter and process until combined, about 30 seconds.

3. With the machine running, add the yolks, one at a time, and process until incorporated. Add the water, zest (if using) and vanilla; pulse 3 to 4 times, until combined.

4. Form dough into 2 flat discs. Use immediately, or wrap in plastic and chill in refrigerator until ready to use. Dough should be firm enough to roll.

Recipe courtesy of Ben Newton – from www.cuisinart.com/recipes/desserts/pate-sucree/

Chefnotes

To make this an almond sucrée, substitute 1/3 cup of the all-purpose flour with toasted almonds. Finely grind the almonds by processing 45 seconds, and then add the remaining dry ingredients. Process 10 seconds to sift and follow instructions as stated above.

Apple Pie

Dough for double-crust pie

⅓ cup white sugar

⅓ cup packed brown sugar

¼ cup all-purpose flour

1 teaspoon ground cinnamon

¼ teaspoon ground ginger

¼ teaspoon ground nutmeg

6 to 7 cups thinly sliced peeled tart apples

1 tablespoon lemon juice

1 tablespoon butter

1 large egg white

Sugar and cinnamon

1. Preheat oven to 375 ° F.
2. On a lightly floured surface, roll one half of dough to a 1/8-in.-thick circle; transfer to a 9-in. pie plate.
3. In a small bowl, combine sugars, flour and spices and set aside.
4. In a large bowl, toss apples with lemon juice. Add sugar mixture to apples and toss to coat.
5. Add the filling to the pie pan and dot with the butter.
6. Roll remaining dough to a 1/8-in.-thick circle. Place over the filling. Trim, seal and flute the edge. Cut slits in the top of the pie.
7. Beat egg white until foamy and brush over the crust. If desired, sprinkle with sugar and cinnamon.
8. Cover edge loosely with foil.
9. Bake in preheated oven for 25 minutes then remove foil from the edge and bake until crust is golden brown and filling is bubbly, about an additional 20 to 25 minutes. Cool and serve. Best served warm with ice cream (in my opinion).

Recipe courtesy of Ben Newton – from www.tasteofhome.com/recipes/apple-pie/

Mom Frank's Pie Crust

I used to think pies were pointless and there were so many desserts I would rather eat. Then I tried my mother in laws pies! Her crust is amazing! She always has extra crust and makes pie crust cookies by baking it with cinnamon and sugar on top.

For one single pie or 4 to 6 tart shells:

1½ cups sifted all-purpose flour

½ teaspoon salt

½ cup shortening

4 to 5 tablespoons cold water

For one 8, 9, or 10-inch double crust or lattice top pie, two 8,9, or 10 inch single crust pies or 6 to 8 tart shells:

2 cups sifted all-purpose flour

1 teaspoon salt

⅔ cup shortening

5 to 7 tablespoons water

1. Sift flour and salt together; cut in shortening with pastry blender till pieces are the size of small peas. (For extra tender pastry, cut in half the shortening till like cornmeal, cut in remaining till like small peas.)

2. Sprinkle 1 Tablespoon water over part of the mixture. Gently toss with fork; push to the side of the bowl. Repeat till all is moistened.

3. Form into a ball, or for double crust and lattice top pies, divide dough for lower and upper crusts and form into two balls.

4. Flatten on lightly floured surface by pressing with edge of hand 3 times across in both directions. Roll from the center to edge till 1/2 inch thick.

5. **For single-crust pie shells:** Fit pastry into pie plate; trim 1/2 inch to 1 inch beyond the edge; fold under the flute edge by pressing dough with forefinger against wedge made of finger and thumb of other hand. Prick bottom and sides well with fork. (If filling and crust are baked together, do not prick.)

6. Bake at 450° F for 10 to 12 minutes or until golden.

7. **For lattice top pie:** Trim lower crust 1/2 inch beyond edge of pie plate. Roll remaining dough 1/8 inch thick. Cut strips of pastry 1/2 to 3/4 inch wide with pastry wheel or knife. Lay strips on filled pie at 1 inch intervals. Fold back alternate strips as you weave cross strips. Trim lattice even with outer rim of pie plate; fold lower crust over strips. seal; flute edge.

8. For double-crust pie: Trim lower crust even with rim of pie plate. Cut slits in top crust. Lift pastry by rolling it over rolling pin; then unroll loosely over well filled pie. Trim 1/2 inch beyond edge. Tuck top crust under the edge of lower crust. Flue edge of pastry as desired.

9. If edge of crust browns too quickly fold strip of foil around rim of crust, covering fluted edge.

Recipe courtesy of Rose Frank – from MaryLou Frank

Yummy Dessert

1 cup sliced almonds

½ cup butter, melted

1¼ cup all-purpose flour

1 8-ounce package cream cheese

2 cups powdered sugar

1 16-ounce package of Cool Whip, divided

1 large (5.1-ounce) package instant vanilla pudding

1 large (5.9-ounce) package instant chocolate pudding

4 cups milk

¼ cup sliced almonds

Chocolate candy bar, shaved

1. Preheat oven to 350 ° F.

2. In small bowl mix together almonds, butter and flour. Press crust into the bottom of 9x13 pan and bake in preheated oven for 15 to 20 minutes.

3. In medium bowl mix together cream cheese, powdered sugar and half of (8 ounces) the cool whip. Spread mixture on top of the crust.

4. In a medium bowl mix together vanilla pudding, chocolate pudding, and milk. Combine until thickened. Spread mixture on top of the cool whip mixture.

5. Cover with the remaining cool whip (8 ounces) and sprinkle with sliced almonds and/or candy bar shavings.

6. Refrigerate and serve when chilled.

Recipe courtesy of Sherry Poulsen

Rice Pudding
makes 6 to 8 servings

*R*ice pudding is one of my favorites. It is great to eat warm, or cold, and has so many unique textures and flavors.

3 cups cooked rice

4 cups milk, divided

⅔ cup white sugar

1⅓ cups raisins

½ teaspoons salt

2 tablespoons butter

2 large eggs, beaten

1 teaspoon vanilla extract

Dash nutmeg or cinnamon, optional

1. Combine rice, 3 cups of milk, sugar and salt in a large saucepan.

2. Cook over medium heat, stirring occasionally until thick and creamy, about 15 to 20 minutes.

3. Beat together remaining cup of milk and eggs.

4. Beat egg mixture into rice mixture.

5. Mix in raisins. Cook 2 minutes longer, stirring occasionally.

6. Mix in butter and vanilla.

7. Remove from the heat and spoon into serving dishes right away.

8. Serve sprinkled with nutmeg and/or cinnamon, if desired.

Recipe courtesy of Ben Newton – from Robyn Walton, rec.food.recipes 1995

Food for Thought

Erin suggests leaving out the raisins

Ben's Vanilla Custard

makes 6 to 8 servings

On my mission in Ireland we were sometimes treated to warm custard for dessert. Custard is so common in Great Britain and Ireland that you can buy it at the store ready-to-serve in cans. Instead of having ice cream with cake, they would often instead serve it with warm custard. My family loves making and eating custard. My kids get tired of many other things I make, but they always ask me to make them custard and cheer when I agree.

4 large eggs, beaten
4 tablespoons cornstarch
4 cups milk
2/3 cup white sugar
2 teaspoon vanilla extract
Frozen berries, chocolate chips, or other toppings, optional.

1. In a large bowl beat eggs, and set aside.

2. Measure cornstarch into a tiny bowl. Measure your first cup of cold milk and from it pour about a tablespoon into the corn starch. Stir to combine. Repeat, alternating adding milk and stirring until you have added about 1/3 cup of the milk and have a lump-free corn starch slurry.

3. In a large saucepan add the reset of the milk from the cup as well as 3 more cups of milk (for a total of 4 cups). Whisk in sugar and the cornstarch slurry and bring to a boil stirring constantly while touching the whisk to the bottom of the pan to stop the mixture from collecting or burning on the bottom of the pan. Remove from heat immediately when it starts to boil.

4. In this step you will temper the eggs to avoid making scrambled eggs. It might be more easily completed with an extra set of hands, (perhaps some of those hands whose mouths are salivating, dreaming of custard.) Using a measuring cup, scoop up some of the hot milk. Pour about 2 tablespoons of the hot milk into the beaten eggs and quickly mix it into the eggs whisking constantly. Continue adding the hot milk to the eggs, whisking all the while, until you've mixed in about 2 cups.

5. Now move the whisk back to the saucepan, which should be still removed from the heat. Introduce the egg mixture into milk mixture in a slow stream, whisking the milk mixture constantly. Continue to whisk until the eggs are completely integrated with the milk.

6. Immediately return the pan to heat and whisk until the custard thickens and begins to spat hot custard, about another two or three minutes.

7. Remove pan from heat and stir in vanilla.

8. You can pour the custard into small bowls and refrigerate for cool custard, but who would want to eat it cold. Serve hot over cake, or by itself with various toppings. Be careful, it is very hot initially. We usually allow everyone to spoon some from the pot into their bowl, and then stir in frozen berries, which cool off the custard as they melt into it. We find that smaller berries, such as blueberries, raspberries, and blackberries work best. Whole strawberries are too big to thaw quickly in the custard. You can also stir in some chocolate chips as they melt for a wonderful chocolate custard. Enjoy!

Recipe courtesy of Ben Newton – adapted from www.food.com/recipe/basic-vanilla-custard-344870

👨‍🍳 Because you are mixing hot milk with eggs, one must be especially careful not to end up with scrambled eggs. To ensure this, it is important to temper the eggs as described above. This recipe requires lots of stirring with a wire whisk. If your arm isn't tired by the end, you didn't stir enough! The directions above describe how I make the custard. If this method doesn't work for you, consider following the directions in the original recipe, linked above.

Strawberry Carrot Dirt Cup
makes 12 servings   prep time: 40 minutes

1 (12-ounce) package orange candy melts, or white chocolate chips and orange food coloring

12 medium-large strawberries

2 (5.9-ounce) packages instant chocolate pudding

6 cups milk

1½ cups crushed Oreos, without the cream

12 (8-ounce) clear plastic cups

1. In a large microwave-safe bowl, melt orange candy according to package directions.

2. Holding each strawberry by its green stem, making sure you don't miss any leaves, dip

3. in orange melted candy so the entire red portion of the berry is covered.

4. Place on wax paper to set. Squeeze extra melted orange candy on top of each dipped strawberry by pouring leftover mixture into a small plastic bag and snipping off a small corner of the bag.

5. In a large bowl mix together instant pudding and milk according to package directions. Evenly distribute pudding between 12 clear cups and let it set up for about 5 minutes.

6. Sprinkle finely crushed Oreos on top of each cup of pudding.

7. Lay a covered strawberry on top of the Oreos in each cup.

Recipe courtesy of Libby Newton

Chefnotes

👨‍🍳 Make sure you have clear cups or bowls so you can see the dirt (pudding).

Crepes
makes makes about 6 crepes

Crepes are one of my favorites. I often ask my dad to make them for dessert. Fill them with any combination of yummy fillings.

½ cup milk, warmed

2 large eggs

½ cup water

¼ teaspoon salt

2 tablespoons butter, melted

¾ to 1 cup all-purpose flour

2 tablespoons white sugar, optional

1 teaspoon vanilla extract, optional

Savory fillings: ham, roast beef, bacon, cheese, ranch, etc

Sweet fillings: pudding, custard, lemon curd, whipped cream, Nutella, etc.

1. Warm milk for 20 to 30 seconds in the microwave.

2. Place all the ingredients in a blender. For dessert crepes include sugar and vanilla, for savory crepes leave out. Blend until smooth, adjusting the amount of flour as needed to get a silky smooth batter the consistency of heavy cream.

3. Heat a lightly oiled griddle or frying pan over medium high heat. Pour or scoop the batter onto the griddle, using approximately 1/4 cup for each crepe. Pick up the pan and tilt it with a circular motion or in various directions so that the batter spreads out on the surface evenly.

4. Cook the crepe for about 2 minutes, until the bottom is light brown. Loosen with a spatula, turn and cook the other side. Serve hot filled with your choice of savory or sweet fillings.

Recipe courtesy of Emma Newton – adapted from www.allrecipes.com/recipe/16383

Food for Thought

Can mix the ingredients in a large bowl instead of the blender, if desired.

Double the recipe to make dinner and dessert for 3 adults and 2 children. If using batter for both savory and then sweet crepes, double the recipe but leave out the sugar and vanilla. After making the savory crepes add the single recipe amounts of sugar and vanilla and use that sweet batter for dessert. 1/4 cup of batter contains about 15 grams of carbohydrates.

Grandma's Cinnamon Rolls

1 recipe of Grandma's Rich Rolls (see page 71)

½ cup butter, softened

1 cup brown sugar

1½ tablespoons cinnamon

White sugar

1. Roll rich roll dough after first proof into an oblong 1/2 in thick.

2. Spread butter on the surface, then sprinkle with brown sugar, cinnamon, and white sugar.

3. Roll, jelly roll style and seal the edges.

4. Cut into slices about 1 1/2 inches wide rolls and place in greased 9x13 in pan. Let double in bulk.

5. Bake on the middle rack at 375 ° F for 20 to 25 minutes.

6. Rolls should be golden brown and the sugars caramelized and bubbling. Turn over on foil and let cool. Carefully scrape sides and bottom of pan to get all the caramel on the rolls, being very careful not to burn yourself.

Recipe courtesy of Deborah Robinson

Chefnotes

☞ Measurements of the sugars and cinnamon are approximate, because I don't usually measure them.

Jen's Cinnamon Rolls

When I was a teenager I went with my mom to a Relief Society activity and learned how to make these cinnamon rolls. I can still remember standing out in the hall, where the kitchen doors opened up, watching the lady from Becki Sue's teach us how to make these. I have been making them for my family ever since then. They truly are a family favorite and requested by my family all the time. They are so soft and delicious and if my dad ever gets ear that I am making these I have to deliver a few to him.

2 tablespoons yeast
½ cup warm water
½ cup white sugar
½ cup vegetable oil
½ teaspoon salt
3 large eggs
1 cup very warm water
5½ cups all-purpose flour
8 tablespoons butter or margarine
Cinnamon
Brown sugar
Frosting:
½ cup soft butter or margarine
3 cups powdered sugar
1½ teaspoons vanilla extract
2 tablespoons milk, approximate

1. In the bowl of stand mixer, dissolve yeast in warm water. Mix in sugar, oil, salt, and eggs.

2. Using a dough hook attachment, add another cup of very warm water and flour. Mix until dough doesn't stick to the sides of the bowl and is smooth and elastic.

3. Transfer dough to a flowered surface and roll into a rectangular shape to desired thickness.

4. Spread generously with butter or margarine.

5. Sprinkle generously with cinnamon, and crumble brown sugar on top.

6. Add nuts or raisins, if desired.

7. Roll into tight jelly roll and cut into desired thickness.

8. Place on a greased baking sheet.

9. Cover and let rise in a warm place till rolls have doubled in size.

10. Preheat oven to 400 ° F.

11. Bake for 10 to 13 minutes.

12. To make frosting, in a medium-sized bowl beat butter, powdered sugar, vanilla and milk until smooth and easy to spread.

13. Frost cinnamon rolls while they are still slightly warm.

Recipe courtesy of Jen Burge – from Becki Sue

Caramel Dip

½ cup margarine

2 cups brown sugar

1 cup corn syrup

2 tablespoons water

1 (14 -ounce) can sweetened condensed milk

1 teaspoon vanilla extract

1. In a saucepan melt margarine. Add brown sugar, corn syrup, and water and bring to a boil.

2. Stir in sweet and condensed milk and stir until thread stage or 220° F. (about 5 minutes).

3. Remove from heat and stir in vanilla.

Recipe courtesy of Sherry Poulsen

Hot Fudge Sauce
makes about two cups

*E*rin brought some of this hot fudge home from a church activity once, along with the recipe. Very dangerous stuff!

⅔ cup heavy cream

½ cup light corn syrup

⅓ cup packed dark brown sugar

¼ cup unsweetened Dutch-process cocoa powder

¼ teaspoon salt

6 ounces fine-quality bittersweet chocolate (not unsweetened), finely chopped

2 tablespoons unsalted butter

1 teaspoon vanilla extract

1. Bring cream, corn syrup, sugar, cocoa, salt, and half of chocolate to a boil in a 1 to 1 1/2-quart heavy saucepan over moderate heat, stirring, until chocolate is melted. Reduce heat and cook at a low boil, stirring occasionally, 5 minutes, then remove from heat. Add butter, vanilla, and remaining chocolate and stir until smooth. Serve once sauce has cooled slightly.

Recipe courtesy of Ben Newton – from www.epicurious.com

Food for Thought

Can refrigerate in an airtight container and reheat to serve.

Grandma Nancy's Road Tar

This is an ice cream topping that the Poulsens had all the time at Winterton family parties. If there was ice cream involved, you knew there would be road tar. It is nice and smooth as you pour it over your ice cream but as it hits the cold it quickly turns to a tar like consistency. Don't worry, it tastes delicious.

2 tablespoons butter

¼ cup cocoa

1 cup water

2 cups white sugar

2 tablespoons corn syrup

Dash of salt

1 teaspoon vanilla extract

1. In a heavy cooking pot, melt butter, then mix in cocoa.

2. Add water, sugar, corn syrup, and salt. Using a wooden spoon and candy thermometer, heat and cook the mixture, stirring often, until it reaches 220° F.

3. Once it reaches that temperature, take the pot off the heat and stir in the vanilla.

Recipe courtesy of Sherry Poulsen – from Grandma Nancy Winterton

Ben's Scones

makes 12 scones   prep time: 15 minutes   cook time: 15 minutes   total time: 30 minutes

These are British scones, not deep fried dough, but a small cake that is moist and soft inside and crumbly on the edges. I made these scones once for Erin's book group. All the ladies loved them, and I earned a lot of brownie points, I means scone points, that night.

1 cup sour cream

1 teaspoon baking soda

4 cups all-purpose flour

1 cup white sugar

2 teaspoons baking powder

¼ teaspoon cream of tartar

1 teaspoon salt

1 cup (2 sticks) butter

1 large egg

1 cup raisins, optional

1. In a small bowl, combine the sour cream and baking soda, and set aside.

2. Preheat oven to 350 ° F. Lightly grease a large baking sheet.

3. In a large bowl, mix the flour, sugar, baking powder, cream of tartar, and salt. Cut in the butter. Stir the sour cream mixture and egg into the flour mixture until just moistened. Mix in the raisins, if using.

4. Turn dough out onto a lightly floured surface, and knead briefly. Roll or pat dough into a 3/4 inch thick round. Cut into 12 wedges, and place them 2 inches apart on the prepared baking sheet.

5. Bake 12 to 15 minutes in the preheated oven, until golden brown.

Recipe courtesy of Ben Newton – from www.allrecipes.com/recipe/20163

Chefnotes

Can brush the scones with 2 tablespoons whipping cream, and sprinkle with sugar before baking. Erin suggests using blueberries, lemon zest, or orange zest instead of raisins.

Index

www.ingramcontent.com/pod-product-compliance
Lightning Source LLC
Chambersburg PA
CBHW061959090426
42811CB00006B/987